"What is particularly impressive about the book is its multidisciplinary coverage, which includes not only linguistics but also classical rhetoric, composition studies, and cognitive science. Equally impressive is that the book covers not only student, instructor, and researcher perceptions about flow in writing but also empirical data to buttress its case. Unsubstantiated perceptions and feelings about improving student writing improvement are no match for empirical evidence, something which this book does not neglect. I believe the book offers very helpful guidance for writing theorists, writing instructors, and students seeking to master the craft of writing."
Rei R. Noguchi, *author of Grammar and the Teaching of Writing:*
Limits and Possibilities (1991)

"This book tackles that most nebulous and desired of writing qualities: *flow*. Refusing to let *flow* continue to be bandied about but little understood, the book offers an accessible investigation of *flow* from rhetorical, linguistic, and cognitive perspectives; then, it offers practical activities to help all of us better identify, understand, and incorporate *flow* in written English."
Laura Aull, *Associate Professor and Writing Program Director,*
University of Michigan, USA

"This book offers a conceptually rich and empirically grounded answer to the thorny question, 'What is flow in writing?' It provides a wealth of insights, strategies, and examples that can help teachers and students to recognize, improve, and even experiment with flow. The authors have me convinced that more focus on flow can reinvigorate the writing classroom and increase students' sense of agency as communicators. I am excited to use this text to help deepen the understanding of students, faculty, writing center staff, and others about how and why flow actually 'works' in written texts!"
Shawna Shapiro, *Associate Professor of Writing and Linguistics,*
Middlebury College, USA

A Multidisciplinary Exploration into Flow in Writing

Offering a multidisciplinary exploration of "flow" and the often-nebulous ways it is conceptualized and operationalized in writing pedagogy, this book addresses a critical gap in writing studies.

Bringing together practice-based and scholarly perceptions, it outlines the key features and definitions of flow, and identifies pedagogical approaches and opportunities for classroom instruction. Incorporating perspectives from disciplines including classical rhetoric, composition studies, cognitive science, and linguistics, this book provides a diverse overview of the literature on flow in writing pedagogy. It includes two instructional voice-based and rhetorical grammar-based activities that outline how to recognize and improve flow in writing. In doing so, the book also provides clear examples of how to create an inclusive writing pedagogy that incorporates sensory and analytical perspectives to help readers and writers experience flow and meet their writing goals.

As an exploration of flow instruction as it currently stands and might stand in the future, this book will be of interest to students and instructors in the field of academic, professional, and creative writing studies.

Deborah F. Rossen-Knill is Executive Director and Professor of Instruction in the Writing, Speaking, and Argument Program at the University of Rochester, USA, and coauthor of a *Guidebook to Academic Writing: Communicating in the Disciplines* (Routledge, 2024).

Katherine L. Schaefer is Professor of Instruction in the Writing, Speaking, and Argument Program at the University of Rochester, USA.

Matthew W. Bayne is Associate Professor of Instruction in the Writing, Speaking, and Argument Program at the University of Rochester, USA.

Whitney Gegg-Harrison is Associate Professor of Instruction in the Writing, Speaking, and Argument Program at the University of Rochester, USA.

Dev Crasta is Senior Instructor in the Department of Psychiatry at the University of Rochester Medical Center, USA.

Alessandra DiMauro is a PhD candidate in Cancer Biology at Washington University in St. Louis, USA.

Routledge Research in Writing Studies

A Writing Center Practitioner's Inquiry into Collaboration
Pedagogy, Practice, And Research
Georganne Nordstrom

Engaging Research Communities in Writing Studies
Ethics, Public Policy, and Research Design
Johanna L. Phelps

Writing, Imitation, and Performance
Insights from Neuroscience Research
Irene L. Clark

Emotional Value in the Composition Classroom
Self, Agency, and Neuroplasticity
Ryan Crawford

Dialogic Editing in Academic and Professional Writing
Engaging the Trace of the Other
Edited by Özüm Üçok-Sayrak, Janie Harden Fritz and Kristen Lynn Majocha

A Multidisciplinary Exploration into Flow in Writing
Deborah F. Rossen-Knill, Katherine Schaefer, Matthew W. Bayne, Whitney Gegg-Harrison, Dev Crasta, and Alessandra R. Dimauro

For more information about this series, please visit: www.routledge.com/Routledge-Research-in-Writing-Studies/book-series/RRWS

A Multidisciplinary Exploration into Flow in Writing

Deborah F. Rossen-Knill,
Katherine L. Schaefer, Matthew W. Bayne, Whitney Gegg-Harrison,
Dev Crasta and Alessandra DiMauro

NEW YORK AND LONDON

First published 2024
by Routledge
605 Third Avenue, New York, NY 10158

and by Routledge
4 Park Square, Milton Park, Abingdon, Oxon, OX14 4RN

Routledge is an imprint of the Taylor & Francis Group, an informa business

© 2024 Deborah F. Rossen-Knill, Katherine L. Schaefer, Matthew W. Bayne, Whitney Gegg-Harrison, Dev Crasta and Alessandra DiMauro

The right of Deborah F. Rossen-Knill, Katherine L. Schaefer, Matthew W. Bayne, Whitney Gegg-Harrison, Dev Crasta and Alessandra DiMauro to be identified as authors of this work has been asserted in accordance with sections 77 and 78 of the Copyright, Designs and Patents Act 1988.

The Open Access version of this book, available at www.taylorfrancis.com, has been made available under a Creative Commons Attribution-Non Commercial-No Derivatives (CC-BY-NC-ND) 4.0 license.

Trademark notice: Product or corporate names may be trademarks or registered trademarks, and are used only for identification and explanation without intent to infringe.

Library of Congress Cataloging-in-Publication Data
Names: Rossen-Knill, Deborah F., author. | Schaefer, Katherine L., 1966– author. | Bayne, Matthew W., 1983– author. | Gegg-Harrison, Whitney, 1983– author. | Crasta, Dev, 1988– author. | DiMauro, Alessandra, 1998– author.
Title: A multidisciplinary exploration into flow in writing / Deborah F. Rossen–Knill, Katherine L. Schaefer, Matthew W. Bayne, Whitney Gegg-Harrison, Dev Crasta, Alessandra DiMauro.
Description: New York, NY : Routledge, 2024. | Series: Routledge research in writing studies ; vol 14 | Includes bibliographical references and index. |
Identifiers: LCCN 2023059310 | ISBN 9781032604954 (hardback) | ISBN 9781032604961 (paperback) | ISBN 9781003459460 (ebook)
Subjects: LCSH: English language—Rhetoric—Study and teaching (Higher) | Academic writing—Study and teaching (Higher) | Interdisciplinary approach in education. | Authorship—Psychological aspects. | Authorship—Technique.
Classification: LCC PE1404 .R678 2024 | DDC 808/.0420711—dc23/eng/20240108
LC record available at https://lccn.loc.gov/2023059310

ISBN: 978-1-032-60495-4 (hbk)
ISBN: 978-1-032-60496-1 (pbk)
ISBN: 978-1-003-45946-0 (ebk)

DOI: 10.4324/9781003459460

Typeset in Times New Roman
by Apex CoVantage, LLC

Deb dedicates this book to Dave Knill, her late husband, and Jack Rossen, her late father. Both were exceptionally clean thinkers—models for academic work—with a jazzy sense of flow.

Finally, we dedicate this to our colleagues and students. We do this for them.

Contents

	Acknowledgments	*x*
	Introduction: A Multidisciplinary Exploration into Flow in Writing	1
1	What Do Scholars Say?	3
2	What Do College Students Say?	43
3	What Do Instructors Say?	65
4	What Do Research Team Members Say?	74
5	Conclusion: What Is Flow in Writing?	90
	Appendix	*95*
	Index	*122*

Acknowledgments

Our first thanks go to the department chairs, office staff, faculty, and students who participated in our study of approaches to teaching flow in writing. Without them, this book would not exist. We are also especially grateful to Peter Elbow, who reviewed our voice-based instructional materials and whose pedagogical work provided a crucial theoretical framework for these materials. A special thanks as well to the Language, Linguistics, and Writing Standing Group and the Progressive Grammar Special Interest Group of the College Conference on Composition and Communication with creating a welcoming intellectual space for linguistic scholars concerned the teaching of writing. These groups inspire and motivate the ongoing collaboration between language study and writing pedagogy.

We are also grateful for the invaluable work of our undergraduate research assistants, Caitlin Davie, Agatha Milholland, and Marin Takikawa. Additionally, we deeply appreciate the work of our copyeditors, Eric Kukenberger and Alexana Dubois. Deb thanks her steadfast writing group partner, Josephine Seddon, for keeping the writing going. A special thanks as well to the University of Rochester for creating a space where writing matters and for providing the resources that made this work and an open-access version of this text possible.

Introduction
A Multidisciplinary Exploration into Flow in Writing

Writers and readers yearn for flow; instructors sense its presence or absence—but they lack a coherent definition of it and the elements that create or disrupt flow. This gap is due, at least in part, to the often-nebulous ways it is conceptualized and operationalized in writing pedagogy. *A Multidisciplinary Exploration into Flow in Writing* addresses this critical gap. Working toward an inclusive, coherent, and pedagogically useful description of flow, this text considers these questions about flow from multiple perspectives: What are the elements of flow? What elements have been identified by different disciplines? What elements do writing instructors, researchers, and students identify when they talk about flow?

In this book, we answer these questions through a multidisciplinary lens. As authors, we draw on our backgrounds in English, computational linguistics, language philosophy, brain and cognitive science, biology, and psychology. We review the literature on flow in writing pedagogy from disciplines as diverse as classical rhetoric, composition studies, cognitive science, and linguistics. In addition, we draw on findings from our study, which investigated instructional approaches for teaching flow in writing. This mixed-method study involved writing courses across two private colleges in the Northeastern United States and aimed to evaluate two different approaches to teaching flow: One approach, inspired by Peter Elbow's work, focuses on voice and performance (e.g., Elbow, 2012; Elbow & Belanoff, 2000), and the other approach, inspired by theories of rhetorical grammar, is analytical (e.g., Hancock, 2005; Kolln & Gray, 2017; Noguchi, 1987, 1991; Rossen-Knill, 2011, 2013). As part of the study, we aimed to learn first-year writing students' ideas about flow before they enter a college writing classroom, using information we gathered through pre-surveys. We also sought to understand instructors' perspectives on flow and their preferred instructional strategies for teaching flow. To this end, we administered pre-surveys and post-surveys and interviewed instructors. Recognizing that we ourselves were significant participants influencing the study, we maintained a record of our process of developing the assessment criteria. We consider this process and the resulting criteria sources of data for the study itself. Ultimately, the flow study generated a rich body of data that revealed students', instructors', and researchers' perceptions about flow in writing.

In *A Multidisciplinary Exploration into Flow in Writing*, we bring into conversation voices from different perspectives, from different stakeholders—scholars, college students, their instructors, and this study's researchers. Together, these voices provide a concrete (and multifaceted) picture of how flow has been conceptualized across fields and how it is conceptualized in real time in the classroom. The emphasis throughout is on pedagogy. We begin with a review of the literature in disciplines that relate directly to teaching flow in writing, most notably composition, rhetoric, cognitive science, and linguistics. The next three chapters present, in turn, perspectives on flow from students, writing instructors, and the researchers. In each of these chapters, we include a methods section (as opposed to a separate methods section for the book as a whole). We do this not only because the data collection varies with the group represented in each chapter but also because the perspectives that emerge are best understood alongside a transparent description of how we came to understand these perspectives. The book's final chapter highlights the common themes coming out of the perspectives presented in each preceding chapter in order to distill key features that underscore the conceptual singularity of flow and identify optimal areas for instruction on flow in writing. Finally, the Appendix provides educators and their students with a voice-based and rhetorical grammar approach for evaluating and improving flow in writing.

References

Elbow, P. (2012). *Vernacular eloquence: What speech can bring to writing*. Oxford University Press.

Elbow, P., & Belanoff, P. (2000). *Sharing and responding* (3rd ed.). McGraw-Hill Higher Education.

Hancock, C. (2005). *Meaning-centered grammar: An introductory text*. Equinox.

Kolln, M., & Gray, L. (2017). *Rhetorical grammar: Grammatical choices, rhetorical effects*. Pearson.

Noguchi, R. R. (1991). *Grammar and the teaching of writing: Limit and possibilities*. NCTE.

Noguchi, R. R. (2002). Rethinking the teaching of grammar. *The English Record, 52*(2), 22–26.

Rossen-Knill, D. F. (2011). Flow and the principle of relevance: Bringing our dynamic speaking knowledge to writing. *Journal of Teaching Writing, 26*(1), 39–67. https://journals.iupui.edu/index.php/teachingwriting/article/view/26270/24281

Rossen-Knill, D. F. (2013). Refining the given-new expectation for classroom use: A lesson in the importance of audience. *Journal of Teaching Writing, 28*(1), 21–51. https://journals.iupui.edu/index.php/teachingwriting/article/view/20717/20250

1 What Do Scholars Say?

Everyone wants flow in writing. When asked what good writing is, instructors and students suggested that "it should 'flow' or hang together" (Aull, 2021, p. 37). Students who visited the writing center regularly asked for help with flow (LeCluyse, 2013; Raymond & Quinn, 2012). In several studies, writing prompts emphasized flow, typically with terms related to paragraph and overall essay organization (Aull, 2015a), and writing instructors graded, implicitly or explicitly, on flow (Aull, 2015a; Knoblauch & Brannon, 1984; North, 2005).

Despite the desire for flow, Peter Elbow observed,

> Many writing teachers hate the term "flow." It's so vague, and when students are asked why they like a certain passage they often settle for saying, "It flows better." But the term is useful because it points to very subtle issues of connection that we can hear but which are hard to analyze.
>
> (Elbow, 2012, p. 225)

Readers, writers, and instructors know it when they feel it. But it remains difficult to define from both conceptual and instructional points of view. It is difficult to identify all of the elements that contribute to flow and how those elements interact in different rhetorical situations, as well as where the boundaries of flow—in contrast to other concerns—begin and end. So what is flow in writing? What elements do researchers, writing instructors, and students articulate when they talk about flow?

In this literature review, we consider these questions from several disciplinary perspectives that have historically informed the teaching of writing. Covering all of the research literature relevant to this question would call for a much longer chapter than this one and risk losing the pedagogical focus of this work. Thus, guided by our primary interest in teaching flow in writing, we have reviewed the work on flow where it is explicitly represented in textbooks for undergraduate and graduates students, on the theory that these textbooks would likely guide most instructors' approaches. As part of that review, we focus on key scholarly works that informed those textbooks.

Next, we review student-facing materials more broadly and examine how flow is (or is not) represented in many popular writing instruction textbooks, undergraduate style guides, student handbooks, or writing center materials. Our overall goal was to identify convergences across perspectives and areas where a consensus has not been reached. (If you have read this far and are curious about materials written explicitly for instructors, see the Appendix for a list of suggestions.)

Because the scope of work on flow is broad and multidisciplinary—a bit like herding cats—we offer here a few comments on how we have framed and organized this material. We have separated this review into two major sections: one focused on rhetoric and composition and the other focused on linguistic approaches. Rhetoric and composition are typically concerned with illuminating larger units of text (e.g., essays or books) and with teaching students how to understand and compose such texts. These areas are heavily influenced by linguistics, cognitive science, and other disciplines (Lunsford & Ede, 1984). Linguistics itself encompasses many overlapping approaches that investigate how relatively small units of text and interaction among textual units represent and create meaning. We have separated rhetoric and composition from linguistic approaches to allow readers to see the different narratives in each of these areas and to recognize that these areas are motivated by different research focuses and methodologies. Of course, this separation is somewhat artificial, and as the literature review points out, some work attends equally to questions of texts and questions of pedagogy. Still, we find this separation of areas a useful approach as it may reflect the experience of researchers, practitioners, and students and so allow them a familiar entry point to this review.

The review also organizes works on flow according to a communication framework, that is, with writers' and readers' perspectives foregrounded. It makes visible the ways in which readers' community memberships and past experiences influence how they come to a text. Notably, this evidence complicates the idea of an undifferentiated reader and similarly complicates the notion of flow as something that a writer can predictably evoke, at least without feedback from readers appropriate to the situation.

Both writers and readers bring a history of language use across many situations and communities, and their abilities and expectations vary based on the situation (Johns, 1997). Simply put, writers do not write in a vacuum; readers do not read in a vacuum. Both writers' and readers' meanings, each influenced by prior experiences, interact to create meaning from a text. Thus, writing is a social act through which meaning is constructed by writers and readers together. It is an act of communication—a rhetorical act.

Importantly, when we discuss flow from a writer-based perspective, we do not mean to suggest that this perspective or the act of writing can have any communicative meaning without the reader. Similarly, focusing momentarily on reader-based perspectives does not mean that the reader's perspective can fulfill a communicative meaning without the writer. At the same time, both in this literature review and sometimes in teaching, it can be helpful to consider separately the writer's and reader's perspectives to explain the processes of writing and reading within the larger context of communication.

Rhetoric and Composition Writing Pedagogies

As Kenneth Burke (1969) said, "the basic function of rhetoric [is] the use of words by human agents to form attitudes or to induce actions in other human agents" (p. 41). Rhetorical approaches focus on people and their interactions with other people: the person trying to influence others and the people listening or reading who might be influenced. In the classical period, this has referred solely to oration and overt one-way argumentation, but the term in modern times has come to refer to analysis of spoken, written, and multimodal language with a range of communicative purposes (Ede & Lunsford, 1984).

Classical rhetoric even today influences much about how we currently think about producing and shaping texts. What writing instructor has not heard of Aristotle's logos, ethos, and pathos? Even those who do not explicitly teach these probably owe something of their instructional approach to at least the first three of Cicero's canons of rhetoric: "invention, arrangement, style, memory, and delivery" (Knoblauch & Brannon, 1984, p. 25). Teaching applications of classical rhetoric, some codified in the early to mid-1800s, have had a strong influence: The rhetorical modes (Newman, 1835) and a focus on paragraph construction including issues of topic sentences, unity, and arrangement (Bain, 1866, as cited in Duncan, 2007) have featured heavily in our teaching.

Early teaching of rhetorical tradition in writing classrooms focused on "ritualized styles of speaking or writing," idealized models of text, and a "mechanistic, skill-based model of composition" (Knoblauch & Brannon, 1984, pp. 25, 80). While this approach could lead to writing that seemed to flow quite well, it limited writers' abilities to communicate in ways that did not fit standardized patterns. In addition, this approach led to student confusion between invention (the process of coming up with ideas) and arrangement (the best way of presenting them) because students were asked to invent in ways that fit the arrangement pattern (Hartwell, 1979; Knoblauch & Brannon, 1984).

In response to these concerns, modern rhetoric took two approaches: one focusing primarily on the process of meaning making by *writers* and the other primarily focusing on the process of meaning making by *readers*. As noted earlier, while we use this distinction to organize our review of the following pedagogies, we recognize that writing and reading are inextricably intertwined. In communication, the writer cannot create meaning without a reader (even when the reader is the writer themselves), and throughout the writing process, the writer often does interact with actual reader-based feedback and/

6 *What Do Scholars Say?*

or an internalized sense of one or more readers. Similarly, the reader's interpretation depends on the writer: The reader makes meaning of a text based on the choices the writer has made in creating the text. It is also worth noting that the concept of a reader or audience is itself complicated. Ede and Lunsford's (1984) "Audience Addressed/Audience Invoked" reflected on how audiences are conceptualized, perceived, created, and interacted with, and the extent to which one can truly have knowledge about the audience's "attitudes, beliefs, and expectations" (p. 156). This work is still regularly cited by authors investigating both rhetoric and writing pedagogy. This topic is one that both rhetoric and composition and the linguistics-based approaches have grappled with in different ways, with consequences for pedagogical approaches. We later discuss the notion of the reader (or the audience) as part of each approach.

Writer-Focused, Organic Pedagogies

Writer-focused pedagogies aim to help writers develop their own writing skills through an organic process of writing and revising. The major claim of these pedagogies is that the process will help writers to develop their ideas clearly and effectively. In this view, flow emerges naturally.

Knoblauch and Brannon's (1984) groundbreaking *Rhetorical Traditions and the Teaching of Writing*, a work that underpins the writer's workshop movement, captured the importance of an organic process centered in the writer's mind:

> Modern rhetoric, by contrast, tries to define the process of composing, not the shapes of texts, assuming that the process is organic, not a series of discrete parts, although it can be analyzed as complementary operations, and assuming that it is in essence a competence, which develops through use, though it also depends on certain skills which are best taught in the framework of developing competence.
>
> (pp. 80–81)

This approach focused on the writer's intentions and meanings and contained a profound respect for the writer's individuality, voice, and innate ability to use language. It also reflected a real concern about a mechanistic approach that broke up writing into a series of discrete skills or parts or focused excessively on "errors" as the main purpose of revision.

In general, process-based approaches posit that writers can develop their ideas naturally, simply by relying on the process: drafting, revising, getting meaningful readers' responses from an audience, reflecting, and engaging the senses through reading out loud (Bizzell, 1992; Elbow, 1998a, 1998b; Elbow & Belanoff, 1989; Emig, 1983; Knoblauch & Brannon, 1984; Murray, 1985; Schultz, 1977). From the point of view of flow, the most striking implication of process-based pedagogies is that an effective structure emerges naturally through the writing process. This idea is perhaps not surprising, given the roots of the process-based approach in rhetoric. As Chaplin (1984) argued, "Rhetoricians have generally conceived of cohesion, unity, and emphasis as a triumvirate firmly embedded in the deep structure of a writer's ideas" (p. vii), although rhetoricians did not specify how this embedding happens. Knoblauch and Brannon (1984) tried to describe a writer-based mental process that might partially explain the phenomenon: "Organization in writing has essentially to do with this ability to discover relationships and convey them as sequences of assertions. The 'composing process,' as modern rhetoric conceives it, is the process of organizing experience through symbolic action" (p. 84). Elbow (1998a) echoed this idea in *Writing With Power*, in a section on initial revisions (after freewriting), where he advocated, "you must insist on finding the ingredients you need in what you've already put on paper. And you must insist on creating the coherence you need by rearranging, not rewriting" (p. 147).

Despite the confidence that an effective structure would emerge as a result of a well-performed writing process, in the early expressions of the writing workshop movement, this perspective was not connected to flow explicitly. The closest these early explorations came to an explicit definition of flow was when Knoblauch and Brannon (1984) talked about "form" in terms of metaphors: "a fabric of argument, a texture of connection, a continuity and directedness of statement" (p. 85). Even as late as 2012, Elbow's *Vernacular Eloquence* referred in passing to flow but did not link it explicitly to organization or ideas.

In actuality, the ideas from modern rhetoric about the process leading to an effective structure are not at all in conflict with traditions from classical rhetoric. Both are concerned with unity, a sense of oneness or how the parts fit together. In the *Poetics*, Aristotle (ca. 350 B.C.E./1994) described a "whole" as an "organic" entity, that is, as "the structural union of the parts being such that, if any one of them is displaced or removed, the whole will be disjointed and disturbed" (Part VIII). This description suggests that unity is related to organization. It also relates unity to cohesion, in some nonspecialized or nontechnical definitions of cohesion: "the act or state of cohering, uniting, or sticking together" (Dictionary.com, n.d., first definition) or "the act or state of keeping together . . . SYNONYM unity" (Oxford Learner's Dictionary, n.d., first definition). Finally, Aristotle's description of unity as "disjointed and disturbed" hints at flow as a sensory experience. However, while Aristotle's description created a picture and experience of flow, it did not specify the elements and related terms that define flow.

Reader-Focused Pedagogies

While the aforementioned writer-focused pedagogies focus primarily on the writer and development of ideas and meaning in the *writer's* mind, it is worth emphasizing that grouping these approaches under a description like "writer's development of ideas or meaning" is somewhat artificial: A large part of a writer's meaning does evolve in response to reader feedback, which is, of course, subject to a reader's process of making meaning. Indeed, multiple key voices within rhetoric and composition, starting with Burke (1974) and Bakhtin (1981), emphasized academic inquiry as a dialogic process. This dialogue may be with writers long dead, with imagined audiences, or with actual readers, but the writer does not write in a vacuum.

Reader-based pedagogies make this dialogue even more explicit and aim to help writers shape their writing by anticipating and responding to the reader's needs. They start from the position that the *reader* is an active (and interactive) participant in making meaning of a text. This means that flow is not something contained solely within the text; it is determined, in part, through the reader's interaction with the text. This idea that readers make meaning is thoroughly embedded in modern rhetoric and composition (Elbow, 1998a; Elbow & Belanoff, 1989, 2000; Knoblauch & Brannon, 1984; Murray, 1985, 2004). However, even with the understanding that the reader plays a role in determining a text's flow, flow has been a slippery concept to pin down.

Linda Flower (1993), in her influential *Problem-Solving Strategies for Writing*, focused on the relationship between the reader and flow, although she also clearly saw the writer as controlling and evaluating some aspects of clarity:

> Because "flow" is such a subjective concept, it is hard to test your own writing for flow as a reader would. What seems clear to you may not seem clear to a reader. . . . Flow, it seems, is a quality that rests in the eye of the beholder. . . . As editors, then, we need a more practical, operational definition of "flow" in order to test our writing from a reader's perspective, not our own.
>
> (p. 284)

While it is clear from Flower's approach that flow has a nebulous, undefined quality and that it derives, in part, from the reader, it is also important to note that she did not explicitly tie it to anything that a reader does. This, as she said, makes the term difficult to operationalize.

The key to this mystery is the reader's mental processing. Chafe (1994), in his *Discourse, Consciousness, and Time: The Flow and Displacement of Conscious Experience in Speaking and Writing*, captured the reader's mental experience and cognitive processing and explicitly tied it to flow. Chafe held up the "metaphor *of flow*, which is intended to capture the dynamic quality of the movement of information into and out of both focal (active) and peripheral (semiactive) consciousness" (p. 30). This definition emphasizes the relationship between the ongoing movement of information through a reader's consciousness to the perception of flow. From this perspective, information may move easily, thus creating flow; conversely, it may be disrupted, creating the familiar perception of a choppy or disjointed text. Chafe's definition also aligns well with Csikszentmihalyi's (1990) psychological understanding of flow as experienced by individuals, a concept that has worked its way both into positive psychology and pedagogical understandings of how to foster learning. Csikszentmihalyi argued that people encounter a flow state when they are concentrating on an intrinsically motivating problem or task that is just at the right level of difficulty; they lose track of time and fail to notice their own conscious thought processes or interruptions. From this perspective, readers may experience flow when they are reading at a level that is neither too difficult nor too easy, are interested in what they are reading, and have information supplied in ways that foster information entering peripheral consciousness at the right time. Parenthetically, it is worth noting that Leahy (1995) applied Csikszentmihalyi's ideas similarly to the concept of writer flow, in much the same way.

All of these definitions implicitly emphasize the reader as an interactive participant who responds to information from the text. However, as Flower noted, it can be hard to anticipate what would make reading a more fluid experience as that depends on what knowledge and expectations readers bring to any given situation. One solution is to focus on meaningful patterns known as schemas, an approach well-illustrated in the pedagogical works of Flower and Hayes (1980), Hartwell (1979), Johns (1997), and Podis and Podis (1990).

All variations of the schema approach argue that particular organizational patterns reduce the cognitive burden on the reader. Schemas have generally been defined as learned organizational patterns: With experience, readers come to develop models of how writing works in the particular situations, languages, and cultures in which they are embedded (Johns, 1986). Familiar or conventionalized organizational patterns are thus essentially genres that grow out of the needs of a particular rhetorical situation and that readers can recognize and use to help make sense of a text. As Miller (1984, p. 155) argued, these patterns are a typified form and action that represent a successful solution to a "Recurrent Rhetorical Situation." For instance, the question–answer schema's organizational approach represents an underlying repetitive exigency (e.g., the need to explain a question and then reason through to the answer) and a set of general expectations that the reader and the writer share (e.g., that the question will come before the answer). On a more complicated level, the move-step framework proposed by Swales (1990, 2004) for introduction–method–result–discussion academic papers (especially introductions and discussions) represents an underlying logic inherent to reporting on an empirical investigation.

Schema approaches capture an important point about the reader's experience: Logic and order of ideas are central to the reader's perceptions. However, using schemas to enhance the reader's perception of flow can be more complicated than it might first seem. Readers are not all alike. In fact, some readers may not be ideal readers (or the author's intended readers) for certain texts—something that every first-year composition instructor who aims to have students read complicated scholarly literature will probably recognize. Readers may well bring the same set of expectations or schemas around problem–solution structures or reporting on an empirical investigation (e.g., Flower, 1993; Johns, 1986), but this may not be enough. They may lack other knowledge (e.g., specific disciplinary, cultural, or situational knowledge) necessary for them to understand a text in a way that aligns with the writer's meaning.

Consider, for example, content knowledge, including knowledge of key vocabulary—a key issue for college-level and early graduate-level readers (and writers!). Failure to understand key terms certainly influenced the reader's perceptions (Beaufort, 2007). Readers also required implicit or explicit knowledge of situation-appropriate ways to organize and express information, including genre and discourse community knowledge (Beaufort, 2007; Bizzell, 1992; Devitt, 2004; Johns, 1997; Swales, 1990). Even if general patterns such as problem–solution or question–answer are understood, this knowledge is often specialized in ways that may not be obvious to someone outside the community, such as a student new to the field. For instance, one might expect both an experienced scientist and a novice student scientist to recognize the common schematic problem–solution expectation to explain how you tested a hypothesis before giving your answer. However, this common schema does not account for accepted variations that students are less likely to have encountered. Explorations of scientific writing for various audiences have shown that the process of investigation is not nearly as clear-cut as the problem–solution schema implies and furthermore—depending on audience and purpose—that there are sometimes very good reasons to start with the answer and work backward (e.g., Bizzell, 1992; Myers, 1990). This issue is why students find it hard to read (and certainly to write) outside one's own area of expertise—something that pedagogical approaches to writing sometimes fail to account for.

A reader's perception of a text is also affected by their facility with the language itself and how textual choices influence shades of meaning (Fitzgerald, 1995). Similarly, a reader's cultural background and expectations for writing can influence how they interpret texts. For instance, Leki (1991), who drew on Kaplan's 1966 explorations of student writing from different cultures and reviewed the work on contrastive rhetoric, offered a model for different writing patterns. This model represents three different reasoning pathways described as "straight line," "zigzags," and "circles" (p. 124). Leki's work shows that explanations of similar texts vary in recognizable ways in different cultures. Notably, both Kaplan and, to a lesser degree, Leki simplified culture-based textual patterns in ways that might obscure important differences within particular cultures. The patterns observed may reflect, in part, the instructional patterns that students were exposed to—which are themselves culturally determined—as well as culturally agreed-on motives for reading and writing (for instance, are you trying to get right to the answer, or do you want to give the reader an interesting puzzle?).

The many aspects that shape the reader's responses—and affect the writer's ability to anticipate the reader's needs—partly explain why student writers have struggled to apply what they have learned in earlier writing situations, including particular genres, to new situations (e.g., Devitt, 2004; Beaufort, 2007). They also underlie many concerns expressed by Wardle (2009) in "'Mutt Genres' and the Goal of FYC." Writing in the first-year classroom often puts the students in an awkward situation as both writers and readers: As *writers*, they are often asked to write an approximation of a genre for a discourse community which they aren't truly part of; as *readers*, they lack some of the necessary content-based and procedural knowledge to make sense of readings. Thus, for all of the reasons described in this section, an instructional approach that teaches students to rely on schemas to anticipate the reader's needs and create flow is, at best, incomplete. Students also need to learn why it is important to get responses from appropriate readers.

Linguistics-Based Pedagogies

Writing instructors who teach from a rhetorical perspective focus heavily on process and on sociocognitive approaches that help writers see how their writing is embedded within particular rhetorical situations and structures. These pedagogies help writers understand that writing and idea development are intertwined and that it is important for writers to be aware of the situation and audience. However, as Aull (2021) noted, these pedagogies do not necessarily leave students with many analytic tools at the sentence level that help them see how textual choices influence the reader, or precisely how or why particular choices sound better or are more effective. In contrast, writing instructors who focus on language pedagogies help students see how textual choices enact qualities that the reader recognizes as contributing to situationally effective prose. These qualities include the ones understood by rhetoric: a sense of a unified, organized whole, cohesion, and emphasis, as well as ones more strongly linked to situational considerations and appropriateness (for instance, consider language usage in a scientific paper vs. a recipe).

These language-focused pedagogies draw heavily on the insights from research fields that investigate spoken or written discourse: discourse studies, functional grammar, pragmatics, and language philosophy. These language-focused fields generally investigate how language is used in context to create meaning, and they typically analyze small units of text (e.g., phrase and clauses). However, the amount of text a researcher investigates varies. In some cases, such as language philosophy, scholars might focus on a few sample sentences (natural or made-up) to unpack how they create particular meanings. In other cases, they might be working from large data corpuses to reveal patterns of language use. While both types of investigation have contributed to language-focused pedagogies, it is worth noting that empirical evidence based on real human communication is key to testing how language is actually used in particular situations. Insights drawn from more anecdotal analyses have been at least partially contradicted by the results of corpus analysis. For example, Graff and Birkenstein's (2010) *They Say/I Say* offered templates that include common phrases used in academic writing. However, through corpus analysis, Lancaster (2016a) determined that the actual use of these phrases across disciplines differed from what *They Say/I Say* suggested.

These fields also share, as a starting point, the view that meaning making is shared, either between participants in a dialogue or between the reader and the writer, as well as the view that making meaning from a text is community- and situation-dependent. This emphasis on textual meaning being created collaboratively and with sensitivity to particular situations is a point of overlap between language-based pedagogies and sociocognitive approaches. However, rhetoric and composition emphasize the writer and the writing process, whereas language-focused pedagogies focus deeply on textual choices.

The language-focused pedagogical approach is probably most famously realized in Williams's highly accessible *Style: Ten Lessons in Clarity and Grace* (1981).[1] In continuous print in one form or another since 1981, this work is enormously influential in writing instruction. Similar approaches are taken by Martha Kolln's *Rhetorical Grammar*, first published in 1991 and currently in its eighth edition (Kolln & Gray, 2017), as well as by Vande Kopple (1989) in *Clear and Coherent Prose: A Functional Approach*, which is, sadly, no longer in print.

These works introduced and defined—sometimes differently—three key concepts relevant to flow: coherence, cohesion, and metadiscourse, as well as general linguistic principles that define how certain textual choices are likely to contribute to coherence and/or cohesion. The works offered a range of overlapping analytical frameworks that allow students to analyze the effects of particular textual choices and craft writing that works as a unified whole and that is more likely to sound good (as the process-based rhetoricians would say) and more likely to reduce cognitive processing load (as the reader-based rhetoricians would say). We next review language-based approaches concerned with coherence, cohesion, and metadiscourse, with an eye toward identifying the theoretical underpinnings of these approaches, areas of confusion, and points of disagreement.

Coherence and Cohesion

Classical and modern rhetoric agree that both ideas and form (or structure) matter. The composition needs to have unity or be an organic whole that works together. As described earlier, Aristotle's idea of the organic whole—if parts are moved or removed, the whole falls apart—suggests an explicit concern for organization (Aristotle, ca. 350 B.C.E./1994, Part VIII). In addition, rhetoric is particularly concerned with cohesion and emphasis, although the concepts are typically not defined or vaguely defined. Over time, language-focused pedagogies have helped clarify these concepts, as well as offer guidance in applying them to improve flow in writing.

Williams's first edition of *Ten Lessons in Clarity and Grace* (1981) offered a limited description of flow that focused on movement across a sentence and avoiding separations that might cause a reader to pause (for instance, a long distance between the subject and the verb). He also vaguely discussed cohesion and coherence, and—strikingly—the index entry for cohesion simply says, "see coherence" (p. 236).

Booth and Gregory's (1987) early work, *The Harper and Row Rhetoric: Thinking As Writing, Writing As Thinking*, captured two ideas about how unity or form and organization might be enacted at the text level:

> Writing must have not only **coherence,** an effective design, but **cohesion,** an explicit set of "hooks" and "ties" that ensure a reader's interest and comprehension. Coherence is the kind of "holding together" that a good design will give any discourse, whether written or spoken. Cohesion is the result of giving readers the right kind of explicit help in *figuring out the design*. Cohesion gives readers the clues for discovering coherence.
>
> (p. 194)

In their definition, coherence was equated to the overall design that creates the sense of a single whole, whereas cohesion involved the cues that enable the reader to make the connections necessary to understand the text as a whole. However, they leave open the question of how localized those connections might be.

Williams's later editions of *Ten Lessons in Clarity and Grace* (various editions, here working from Williams, 2003), which echoed and expanded on Booth and Gregory's (1987) definitions, are among the few writing textbooks that explicitly link cohesion and coherence to flow. Williams referred to coherence on two levels: the larger compositional level, which he termed "globally coherent" (p. 209) and the passage or paragraph level, which he termed "locally coherent" (p. 209).

At the compositional level, Williams (2003) defined coherence in ways that recall rhetoric's definitions:

Readers judge your writing to be globally coherent when they

- see your main point;
- understand the relevance of its parts to that point;
- recognize the principle behind the order of those parts; and
- read it all purposefully and attentively.

(p. 210)

14 What Do Scholars Say?

Much of the book, however, dealt with local concerns. Starting with two sample paragraphs, Williams invited us to sense the difference; he then observed that the first paragraph "feels choppy, even disorganized" (p. 78), noting a sensory effect as well as one explicitly linked to the organization. He argued that the paragraphs make the reader feel that the writing is unfocused and defined two constituent terms that influence this feel:

- We judge sequences of sentences to be *cohesive*, depending on how each sentence ends and the next one begins.
- We judge a whole passage to be *coherent*, depending on how all the sentences in the passage cumulatively begin.

(pp. 78–79)

He then followed up with a definition of coherence which echoes unity: "A SENSE OF THE WHOLE" (p. 83), and further suggested that we differentiate cohesion and coherence in this way:

- Think of *cohesion* as the experience of seeing pairs of sentences fit neatly together, the way two Lego® pieces do.
- Think of *coherence* as the experience of recognizing what all the sentences in a piece of writing add up to, the way lots of Lego® pieces add up to a building, bridge, or boat.

(p. 83)

This definition of coherence aligns with Booth and Gregory's (1987) definition, as well as concepts from rhetoric, in that coherence involves maintaining an overall main point or idea. However, Williams extends the idea by suggesting that coherence involves not only thematically connected ideas, but also the progression of ideas—things that "add up to" (p. 83) a major point. This definition of cohesion, or the Lego model, suggests that the explicit hooks and ties have to do with how the sentences fit together.

Williams's (2003) work was enormously influenced by systemic functional linguistics, a branch of linguistics that analyzes real-world language use in order to describe how the discourse context—including those involved, their purpose, and the situation—relates to linguistic choices. In particular, Williams drew heavily from Halliday and Hasan's (1976) *Cohesion in English*.

Halliday and Hasan (1976) agreed with Williams (2003) that cohesion has to do with connections between sentences. They presented an exhaustive description of the ways that writers can execute the sentence-to-sentence connections and sorted them into five categories: reference, substitution, ellipsis, conjunction, and lexis. While their work may seem excruciatingly technical to the non-linguistically minded, some of these concepts, especially reference (referring back to a previously mentioned topic) and lexis (word choice), have worked their way into writing instruction. For one example, see the analysis of King's *Letter from a Birmingham Jail* in Graff and Birkenstein's *They Say/I Say* (second edition; 2010, pp. 114–115) for its use of repeated or related terms as cohesive elements.

The primary difference with Halliday and Hasan (1976) is that they—unlike Williams (2003)—explicitly noted that sentence-to-sentence connections may involve not only adjacent sentences but also connections within sentences and across nonadjacent sentences. They did agree that cohesion is only one part of the larger coherence and that coherence has to do with information, ideas, and themes:

> Cohesion expresses the continuity that exists between one part of the text and another. It is important to stress that continuity is not the whole of texture. The organization of each segment of a discourse in terms of its information structure, thematic patterns and the like is also part of its texture ... no less important than the continuity from one segment to another.
> (p. 299)

Regardless of precisely where the bounds of cohesion begin and end, Williams along with Halliday and Hasan agrees that coherence and cohesion are separate functions. Williams's definition of coherence and cohesion explicitly separates their mechanisms. He related coherence to progression of topics in sentences at the local level and to how the ideas are presented and organized at the global level. In both cases, the progression of easily related ideas determines coherence. In contrast, cohesion is determined by the relationship between adjacent sentences.

Kolln and Gray (2017) also explicitly discussed flow and linked it to cohesion and an implied sense of coherence. Their definition in *Rhetorical Grammar: Grammatical Choices, Rhetorical Effects* aligns, in part, with Williams's *Style: Ten Lessons in Clarity and Grace* (2003). Kolln and Gray defined cohesion in terms of sentence-to-sentence connections but then also suggested that cohesion includes a concept similar to Williams's coherence and rhetoric's conception of unity. However, they did not mention coherence explicitly: "**Cohesion** refers to the connection of sentences to one another, the flow of a text, and the ways in which a paragraph of separate sentences becomes a unified whole" (p. 139).

Whereas Williams (2003) separated the textual choices that add up to cohesion and coherence, focusing on progression of topics when describing coherence, Kolln and Gray (2017) seem to imply that choices that lead to sentence-to-sentence cohesion will also lead or contribute to the sentences adding up to a unified whole. In this, they seem to echo Vande Kopple (1989), who explicitly unified cohesion and coherence and identified them as what Williams would consider cohesion:

> When I use the term *coherence*, I do so to describe prose in which nearly all the sentences have meaningful connections to sentences that appear

both before and after them. The terms *cohesion* and *cohesiveness* would probably work just as well to describe such connections. But I use *coherence* to describe these connections and more.

(Vande Kopple, 1989, p. 3)

It is worth noting, as Williams did, that simple cohesion—while it often does lead to coherence—does not always lead to coherence, emphasizing the need, as Vande Kopple says, for "more" (p. 3). For instance, consider the example that Williams gives (underlines added by us show how Williams's Lego-like interlocking between sentences works):

> Sayner, Wisconsin, is the <u>snowmobile</u> capital of the world. The buzzing of <u>snowmobile</u> engines fills the air, and their tanklike tracks crisscross the snow. The <u>snow</u> reminds me of Mom's <u>mashed potatoes</u>, covered with furrows I would draw with my fork. Her <u>mashed potatoes</u> usually make me sick, that's why <u>I</u> play with them. <u>I</u> like to make a hole in the middle of the <u>potatoes</u> and fill it with melted butter. <u>This behavior</u> has been the subject of long chats between me and my analyst.
>
> (p. 83)

In any event, in addition to reflecting a possibly evolving vocabulary for discussing these subjects, the fluid definitions of coherence probably reflect the use of the term *coherent* to refer to properties that unify a text as a whole (back to unity again!) versus a part of the text (such as a passage or paragraph). Ideas, organization, logical relationships among ideas, and cohesion between sentences all contribute to a sense of coherence, and different analysts' definitions depend on the scope of the texts that they focus on. It probably also reflects the inherent difficulty of separating ideas and organization as they are, to some extent, intertwined—just as the rhetorical approach emphasizes.

Rhetorical Grammar

Operationalizing the ideas reviewed previously, several introductory writing textbooks described how to enact cohesion and coherence in the text. In addition to Williams's *Style: Ten Lessons in Clarity and Grace* (1981, 2003), Vande Kopple's (1989) *Clear and Coherent Prose*, Hancock's (2005) *Meaning-Centered Grammar: An Introductory Text*, and Kolln and Gray's (2017) *Rhetorical Grammar* alerted students to common sentence patterns that could help them achieve a range of effects, including flow. Another recent text suitable for high school, college, and linguistics students, Paraskevas's (2021) *Exploring Grammar Through Texts*, focused explicitly on both reading and writing. Like Williams's works, these pedagogical texts draw on work from systemic functional linguistics (SFL) in relating textual choices to the discourse situations that motivate communication, as do some more specialized textbooks, including Halliday's *An Introduction to Functional Grammar* and its later revision into Halliday and Matthiessen's multiple-edition *Halliday's Introduction to Functional Grammar*, as well as Halliday and Martin's [1993] *Writing Science: Literacy and Discursive Power*. In keeping with SFL's primary concern for how language is used to make meaning in communication, the writing pedagogy texts based on SFL view meaning and communicative purposes as the basis for language choice and language as a rich tool for creating and communicating meaning. This pedagogical approach is captured perfectly by Kolln's title, *Rhetorical Grammar: Grammatical Choices, Rhetorical Effects*. Quite naturally, this area of writing pedagogy has become known as *rhetorical grammar*.

Rhetorical grammar divides the sentence (or clause) into two main focal points—the beginning and the end—and describes different functions for each part. Depending on the approach, the beginning can be thought of as the topic (what this is about), the theme, the sentence's starting point, the subject, or given or known information, while the end is a point of emphasis by default and the position for important new information about the topic (see Vande Kopple, 1991, for a review of the terminology related to first elements of a sentence). While the beginning and end of sentences are described somewhat differently in different frameworks, there is general agreement that readers will look to the beginning of a sentence to know what the sentence is about (the topic) and toward the end to learn the important and/or new information about the topic.

Knowledge about the different functions of the beginning and end of sentences has enabled the articulation of some general principles for how readers or listeners work their way through text or speech interactions. These principles can be used to analyze how textual choices influence how readers are likely to progress through the text and to make connections between parts globally or locally, as well as where they focus their attention. The principles, discussed in more detail in the following paragraphs, include the topic–comment (or theme–rheme) principle, the given-new (or old-before-new) principle, and the principle of end-focus. Three of these principles are intimately related to how readers make sense of sentence-to-sentence connections (cohesion), and at least two principles can also help a writer analyze issues across paragraphs in relation to the overall meaning or unity (coherence).

These approaches are analytic frameworks that help writers achieve particular rhetorical effects (Micciche, 2004)—hence, as noted earlier, the name *rhetorical grammar*. They make generalized statements about how a writer's choices within sentences can influence the reader's perceptions. These principles are based on the analysis of existing samples of well-received texts from a range of genres, written transcriptions of successful dialogue, and occasionally from a reader's or a speaker's intuitions, and extrapolating from the patterns seen in the text to what is going on in a reader's or listener's mind. They should not, however, be seen as "rules" of writing. Instead, they are principles that allow writers to evaluate how well their writing is likely to flow and to analyze reader-reported problems (e.g., see Salvatore, 2021). It is important to note that these principles alone will not bring about flow or create effective texts nor are they universally satisfied in every sentence or utterance of effective texts. In fact, writers might intentionally flout these principles for a particular reason and, as a result, create especially effective texts (see, e.g., discussion of Amis's *Times Arrow* in Rossen-Knill, 2013). Simply put, the writer's purpose and the competing effects of different principles can complicate the picture. Nevertheless, as a pedagogical tool for developing writers' awareness of how their texts work, including how their texts flow, they are a very useful tool.

Focusing on the rhetorical choices and effects related to the beginning of sentences, Williams (2003) argued that the topics of sentences or clauses (and paragraphs, at the larger level) contribute a great deal to coherence. Importantly, it is the progression of topics from one sentence to another that builds coherence:

> **Readers** look for the topics of sentences to tell them what a whole passage is "about." If **they** feel that its sequence of topics focuses on a limited set of related topics, then **they** will feel they are moving through that passage from a cumulatively coherent point of view. But if **topics** seem to shift randomly, then **readers** have to begin each sentence from no coherent point of view, and when that happens, **readers** feel dislocated, disoriented, and the **passage** seems out of focus.
>
> (p. 85)

The reader is able to follow the shifts from "readers" to "they" very easily, and only two clauses start with anything else; all the reader has to do is make the transition to the previously mentioned "topics" and "passage" (and both are linked in another way, the given-new principle, discussed shortly).

Vande Kopple (1989), Halliday and Martin (1993), and Halliday and Matthiessen (2013) similarly noted that sentences could be functionally divided into two parts[2]: The first part is what the sentence is about (called "topic" by Vande Kopple and "theme" by Halliday) and the second part says something about—or comments on—the first part (referred to as "comment" by Vande Kopple and "rheme" by Halliday). Although Vande Kopple and Halliday defined these elements somewhat differently, they agreed that a sequence of easily relatable topics within a paragraph help maintain a sense of coherence: The reader keeps seeing the sentence as being about a topic, and the addition of new information in the comment keeps the paragraph moving along. At the global level, being able to connect adjacent topics clearly, or see thematic progression, allows for a better sense of coherence.

Williams (2003) also explicitly linked cohesion to connections between sentences, specifically pointing to the importance of how one sentence ends and the next one begins. This idea corresponds to two separate but related concepts: given-new and end-focus. The given-new principle indicates that readers expect known or established information to come before new information. Based on systemic functional linguistics (e.g., Halliday & Matthiessen, 2013), this principle has appeared in a few writing textbooks (Hancock, 2005; Kolln & Gray, 2017; Vande Kopple, 1989; Williams, 2003). The principle demonstrates that beginning a sentence with information established in the previous sentence helps the reader make the connection between that previous information and the new information in the following sentence. This given-new principle can help connect adjacent sentences and—depending on how easily the old concept is recalled—sentences across larger distances.

Sometimes the linkage is fairly explicit, as in this example from Kolln and Gray (2017), where the "two researchers worked on projects" is easy to mentally equate with "their collaboration": "The two researchers worked on numerous projects together. Although their collaboration eventually ended, they . . . " (p. 143). In other cases, the linkage is more implicit and relies on inferences based on shared knowledge, as in this example, where the reader has to understand that a trip usually involves a hotel room, new food, and transportation options:

> *Our trip to Florida for spring break* turned out to be a disaster. The hotel room we rented was miserable—shabby and stuffy and utterly depressing. The food we could afford made the cafeteria food on campus seem positively gourmet. The shuttle bus to the beach we had been promised showed up only once and even then was an hour late.
>
> (p. 144)

The given-new approach calls to mind—in much more accessible language—Halliday and Hasan's (1976) categories of ways that sentences can be connected (reference, substitution, ellipsis, conjunction, and lexis), as well as the importance of referring back to familiar or known information.

The end-focus principle can help with both emphasis and cohesion. At the sentence level, it harks back to the notion of emphasis from ancient rhetoric, with the idea that the most important information is found at the end. While ancient rhetoric and its extensions to paragraph theory considered emphasis at multiple levels, the idea that end-focus applied at the sentence level may have been first widely popularized in writing instruction by Gopen and Swan (1990), who applied it (along with the given-new principle) to advice about scientific writing. These examples from Kolln and Gray (2017) show how a simple change in what comes at the end of a sentence can change what the reader focuses on (brackets for focus are ours):

> According to the *Chicago Tribune*, Thomas E. Dewey won the 1948 presidential election [focus on the election]. But correspondent Arthur Sears

Henning made a huge error [focus on the error]. The voters had elected Harry S. Truman [focus is on the person who did win].

According to the *Chicago Tribune*, Thomas E. Dewey won the 1948 presidential election [focus on the election]. But correspondent Arthur Sears Henning made a huge error [focus on the error]. Harry S. Truman had been elected by the voters [focus on the voters].

(p. 158)

In addition to its role in emphasis, the end is important for another reason. It often serves as given in the next sentence and thus brings about the sentence-to-sentence connections that create cohesion.

Pragmatics and Language Philosophy

Insights from pragmatics, while much less integrated into introductory writing instruction, also contain important information about textual cues related to both cohesion and coherence. Pragmatics, as does systemic functional linguistics, investigates how language in use leads to successful communication, that is, communication in which the speaker/writer produces a text to communicate a message and the hearer/reader works out the speaker's/writer's intended message (or, actually, a close approximation of that message). Pragmatics also focuses on the meaning of a particular utterance and the types of procedural and implied knowledge that permit communication to occur (Barron et al., 2017). It is this sort of analysis that belies a once-common piece of writing advice): Write so that you cannot be misunderstood by anyone who would read your writing.

The language philosopher Grice (1989) posited a set of principles and a reasoning process for how meaning is made in conversation. This descriptive framework involves the overarching *cooperative principle*: "Make your conversational contribution such as is required, at the stage at which it occurs, by the accepted purpose or direction of the talk exchange in which you are engaged" (p. 26). Grice elaborated on this principle with four maxims that identify the different dimensions of expected cooperation: quality, relevance, quantity, and manner. For the purposes of explaining how meaning emerges from conversation, Grice assumed a rational speaker and hearer, as well as their understanding that the speaker and hearer enter the conversation with a shared goal and the belief that what is said is relevant. The cooperative principle and the four maxims that follow it make it clear that context matters, that the participants define a shared conversational goal, and that participants cooperate to build a successful conversation. While Grice's work focused on spoken language, or utterances, it has been extended to writing pedagogy (Kuriloff, 1996).

Also concerned with how language—as used in communication—creates meaning, language philosopher J. L. Austin in *How to Do Things With Words* (1975) focused on the "speech act." As its name suggests, the "speech act" captures his observation that "*by* saying something we do something" (p. 91). John Searle, another language philosopher, furthered this work, most notably in *Speech Acts* (1969), in which he laid out a taxonomy of the ways utterances do things in the world and, drawing on Grice, a procedure to account for how listeners work out an utterance's meaning. While Austin's and Searle's work has not been fundamental to writing pedagogy, it does have a central place in Joseph Harris's (2006) writing textbook, *Rewriting: How to Do Things With Texts*.

Sperber and Wilson (1995), grounded in cognitive science, dug into the question of how exactly hearers/readers draw on context to work out a communication's meaning. They argued that the maxim of relation—or in their reformulation, the *principle of relevance*—is fundamental to a hearer being able to work out the meaning of a speaker's utterance. The cooperative principle and the principle of relevance emphasize that human communication is not a matter of decoding a text, but rather a matter of interpretation, one in which the speaker/writer and hearer/reader collaborate to construct a text's meaning. Rossen-Knill (2011), in an article explicitly focused on pedagogy, expanded on this idea and argued that the principle of relevance can "help instructors and students draw on their implicit knowledge as speakers to test and enhance paragraph flow" (p. 42). This approach relies on Sperber and Wilson's development of Grice's (1989) maxim of relevance in conversation: Readers will assume that if information is supplied in a particular place, it must be relevant, and then work hard to make the connections that make the information relevant. If this is easy (i.e., the cognitive load is low), the writing flows; if it is harder and the reader experiences a pause while they try to make connections, flow is interrupted. It is striking how much this idea echoes Booth and Gregory (1987)'s definition of cohesion: "Cohesion is the result of giving readers the right kind of explicit help in *figuring out the design*. Cohesion gives readers the clues for discovering coherence" (p. 194).

The approach based on the principle of relevance is consistent with basic schemas. Additionally, it is consistent with the questions under discussion (QUD) theory of discourse (Beaver et al., 2017; Larsson, 1996; Roberts, 2012). Like the basic schemas of question–answer and problem–solution, the QUD model suggests that in coherent discourse, each new utterance answers a question or concern raised by the preceding sentence or clause. This approach suggests that readers continually vary their expectations as they move forward through the discourse, a supposition that has been supported by empirical evidence (Kehler & Rohde, 2017). It thus seems reasonable to assume that if the utterance did not answer a reader's question, or if the reader had to work hard mentally to make it answer the question that they had, their sense of flow would be interrupted. While this research does not have an explicit presence in writing instruction, a related concept does appear in Rawlins and Metzger's (2009) *The Writer's Way* in their discussion of "Having a Reader in Your Head" (p. 22). This work advised: "Imagine a first-time reader reading it and guess how she responds. The more you hear the reader's responses, the better you can decide how to react to and control them, and the better you'll write" (p. 22). Notably, the examples given of possible (imaginary) readers' responses were heavy on questions, although they also imagined agreement or pushback.

Metadiscourse

Metadiscourse is an important linguistic resource that contributes to a text's sense of cohesion and coherence—both locally and globally—and is thus relevant to flow. In 1985, in the influential *College Composition and Communication* journal, Vande Kopple published his call for more attention to metadiscourse when teaching writing. Vande Kopple built on Williams's 1981 edition of *Style: Ten Lessons in Clarity and Grace*, which offered a beginning definition of metadiscourse as well as a starting taxonomy. Both authors developed their ideas and produced overlapping taxonomies of metadiscourse that have worked their way into writing instruction, as well as inspiring a large body of empirical, corpus-based research.

Several scholars, including Williams (1981 and later editions), Vande Kopple (1989, 1991, 2002, 2012), Aull (2015a, 2015b, 2019, 2021), Aull and Lancaster (2014), Lancaster (2014, 2016a, 2016b), Hyland (1999, 2005, 2011), and Hyland and Tse (2004), developed a body of work, some of which we review here. They proposed and refined definitions and taxonomies of metadiscourse based on different ways that phrases and clauses guide the reader through the text and convey the writer's attitude toward the text's propositional content (e.g., the argument or point being made by the author) and the context beyond the text (e.g., the reader). However, while they may define or categorize types of metadiscourse differently, they all agree that metadiscourse serves an important social function in communication: It is a writer's projection of the reader–writer interaction embedded in the text, a projection that serves to guide and connect with the reader. Metadiscourse provides signals that guide the reader through the text and supplies cues as readers need them to make sense of the text; it also helps build a relationship with the reader. Owing to these functions, it is reasonable to expect metadiscourse to increase the ease with which the reader works through the text and, as a result, their subjective sense of flow.

In his writing text *Clear and Coherent Prose* (1989), Vande Kopple defined metadiscourse using the topic–comment framework described earlier: "Metadiscourse is language that does not appear in topics, does not add information about topics, and therefore does not expand the information about the overall subject of a passage" (p. 55). This is not to say that metadiscourse cannot appear at the beginning of a sentence. It can; it is simply categorized as metadiscourse and not as part of the topic. For clarification, consider this sentence: *However,* **Jay** *did not like chocolate ice cream.* *However* is the metadiscourse that connects the propositional idea in the sentence to previous ideas, **Jay** is the topic, and *did not like chocolate ice cream* is the comment about the topic **Jay**. Characterizing the function of metadiscourse, Vande Kopple stated, "writers do not convey information about the world but direct readers how to read, react to, and recall that information" (p. 55). Vande Kopple went on to categorize metadiscourse into "connectives" (convey how "parts of passages are connected to each other"), "action markers" (convey the writer's action with respect to the type of knowledge, as in *I will prove*), "modality" (conveys the degree of certainty, as in *perhaps or without a doubt*), "narrators" (convey the source of information, as in *according to Mary*), "attitudes" (convey the writer's perspective or feelings toward the topical material, as in *notably*), and finally "commentary" (a direct address to the reader, as in *you might skip this section*) (pp. 55–57). Vande Kopple noted that across his six categories, there is sometimes overlap in function (p. 55).

Williams (2003), in *Style: Ten Lessons in Clarity and Grace*, took a similar approach, but rather than beginning with the topic, he began with the verb, more specifically, with whether the verb was in the passive or active voice. After showing several examples from science writing where either the active or passive voice was used, he noted that there were two types of verbs. In the first type, the passive voice was used when referring to the subject matter or the research, as in "*the subjects* WERE OBSERVED" (p. 66). In contrast, the writer chose the second type, active voice, when referring to their own writing and thinking, as with the verbs cite, show, or inquire in a construction such as "*We* WILL SHOW" (p. 66). He then went on to refer to the metadiscourse functionally: "When you use this second kind of verb to refer to your own thinking and writing, you use what we call *metadiscourse*" (p. 66). He further categorized metadiscourse into categories that overlap with Vande Kopple's: Phrases that have the function of making "logical connections" (similar to Vande Kopple's connectors), those that "show the writer's thinking and writing" (similar to Vande Kopple's certain classes of action markers), words or phrases showing "the writer's degree of certainty" (identical to Vande Kopple), and phrases influencing "the readers' actions" (what Vande Kopple calls commentary) (p. 66).

After publishing *Clear and Coherent Prose*, Vande Kopple refined his taxonomy in ways that brought it closer to Williams' (Vande Kopple, 2002, 2012), but he did not publish an updated version of his writing textbook for students. The 2012 version of his taxonomy (pp. 38–40) pointed to "Text Connectives" (same as his earlier connectives), "Code glosses" (explanations, restatements, or clarifications explicitly linked back to previous statements, as in *what I mean to say is*), "Illocution Markers" that mark rhetorical moves in the writing (e.g., *I hypothesize*), "Epistemology Markers" that convey the writer's level of certainty (e.g., *probably*), and "Attitude Markers" and "Commentary" (both same as in his earlier version). His work was then taken up by Aull and Lancaster, who further refined, expanded, and, in some cases, modified Vande Kopple's terminology slightly.

Both Vande Kopple's (1989) and Williams's (2003) work explicitly stated that through metadiscourse, writers interact with readers. For example, Vande Kopple stated, "Writers let their readers know" (p. 56), and Williams emphasized the writer–reader interaction in the header "Metadiscourse: Writers and Readers as Characters" (p. 66). In addition, they both hinted at two larger categories of metadiscourse: those used to convey attitudes toward the materials (which are not likely to be directly related to flow) and those used to organize and guide the reader (which might be related to flow). However, Vande Kopple and Williams were not explicit about these distinctions in the way that exists in the work of Hyland and colleagues.

Whereas Vande Kopple focused on teaching college writing, Hyland, who has a background in teaching English as another language, focused on teaching undergraduate and graduate students whose first language was not English as part of a broader focus on genre pedagogy (Hyland, 2003, 2007, 2008). Hyland has also called for attention to metadiscourse, and his pedagogical approach suggested instructors to call attention to and ask students to analyze the linguistic features of relevant genres as they are used in the reading and writing of particular discourse communities. This approach was featured in the widely popular *Academic Writing for Graduate Students* by Swales and Feak (2012), who come from the same language pedagogy tradition.

Hyland and colleagues developed a taxonomy similar to the ones described earlier and applied it to the question of how metadiscourse works in a broad range of corpus-based samples of published scholarly written texts across the disciplines. Hyland and Tse (2004), in "Metadiscourse in Academic Writing: A Reappraisal," defined metadiscourse in terms of general functional principles (brackets ours):

1. metadiscourse is distinct from propositional aspects of discourse [Vande Kopple focuses on starting with topics, and Williams starting with verbs];
2. the term "metadiscourse" refers to those aspects of the text that embody writer–reader interactions [in agreement with Vande Kopple and with Willliams];
3. metadiscourse distinguishes relations that are external to the text from those that are internal.

(p. 159)

Their categorization makes an important distinction that Vande Kopple's and Williams's did not: It divided metadiscourse into "interactional resources" (which "involve the reader in the argument") and "interactive resources" (which "help to guide reader through the text") (p. 169). They argued that both types of markers carry out social functions. Through interactional markers, writers convey their perspectives and attitudes and help establish that the writer and reader are part of the same community. These markers included "hedges" (e.g., *conceivably*), "boosters" (e.g., *most surely*), "attitude markers" (e.g., *importantly*), "engagement markers" (e.g., phrases like *as we know*), and "self-mentions" (e.g., *I* or *we*) (p. 169). Through interactive markers, writers guide readers through the text by establishing connections across ideas. These included "transitions" (e.g., *however*), "frame markers" (e.g., *in conclusion*), "endophoric markers" (e.g., *refer to Figure 1*), "evidentials" (e.g., *as Mary notes*), and "code glosses" (explanations that help readers grasp the idea, as in *to put another way*) (p. 169).

In many later expansions of this material starting in 2005, Hyland unpacked further the functions of engagement markers in ways that suggest that at least some of the interactional resources may also influence flow. He noted that coaxing the reader to feel a relationship will also allow writers to "recast knowledge as sympathetic understanding, promoting tolerance in readers through an ethical rather than cognitive progression" (Hyland, 2005, p. 187) or, as Peshe Kuriloff (1996) described in her exploration of reader–writer interactions in text, lead readers to be "content to follow me [the writer] without protest" (p. 492). This might well make passage through a text feel more connected.

Hyland's work further examined how metadiscourse markers functioned in academic writing and compared their use in disciplines from the natural, applied, and social sciences, as well as the humanities (see Hyland, 2011, for a summary of much of this work), showing that writers in different disciplines use metadiscourse in distinctly different ways. Since Hyland, other researchers have investigated metadiscourse and sentence-level patterns of student academic writers at different levels and across different situations (e.g., Aull, 2015a; Aull & Lancaster, 2014). Their body of work supports the idea that the metadiscourse use influences how student writing is received. Higher graded papers included the successful use of more metadiscourse features (Lancaster, 2014), and student papers showed more successful use of these features in later college writing (Aull & Lancaster, 2014; Lancaster, 2016b). Their work also supports the idea that the successful use of metadiscourse depends on genre and disciplinary or discourse community expectations (Lancaster, 2014; Aull, 2019), again underscoring its rhetorical function. This type of work emphasizes an important implication for pedagogy: The frequency and use of markers vary recognizably according to the discipline and situation. This suggests that flow itself, or a reader's experience of flow, is situation-dependent.

While Williams's long-running *Style* is in print and used in undergraduate instruction, Vande Kopple's (now out of print) and Hyland's work (as featured in graduate writing instruction) are much less well-integrated into undergraduate writing instruction. The other major source of textbook instruction on metadiscourse is likely to be Graff and Birkenstein's (many editions, here 2021) of *They Say/I Say: The Moves That Matter in Academic Writing*. This work aligns with parts (but not all) of Vande Kopple's, Williams's, and Hyland's work.

In all editions of *They Say/I Say*, Graff and Birkenstein offered a series of templated phrases that they claimed academic writers use to introduce particular functions in writing—for instance, summarizing, quoting, agreeing or disagreeing, and dealing with objections. As suggested by the text's subtitle, *The Moves That Matter in Academic Writing*, they categorized the phrases in terms of moves, that is, the function that the bit of text performs. The fifth edition (2021) included a chapter on metadiscourse (what they call metacommentary), which they defined this way: "Think of metacommentary as a sort of second text that stands alongside your main text and explains what it means" (p. 139). They also noted that not all of the examples of metacommentary were confined to the metacommentary chapter: "Many of the other moves covered in this book function as metacommentary: entertaining objections, adding transitions, framing quotations, answering 'so what?' and 'who cares?'" (p. 143). While Graff and Birkenstein's discussion of metacommentary did not come with a detailed taxonomy of the kind found in the work of Vande Kopple, Williams, or Hyland, they do roughly seem to agree that metadiscourse involves an aspect that signals the writers' attitude toward the propositional material, as well as one that guides the reader through the material.

While Graff and Birkenstein's approach has intuitive appeal (students can probably categorize moves much as Graff and Birkenstein do), it lacks the precision of the categorizations offered by Williams (2003), Vande Kopple (2012), and Hyland and Tse (2004) and does not give the reader sufficient information to identify particular kinds of metadiscourse and their functions. For instance, in Graff and Birkenstein's (2021) metacommentary chapter, they included as their first major header "USE METACOMMENTARY TO CLARIFY AND ELABORATE" (p. 140). This description might suggest what later Vande Kopple and Hyland and Tse both called "code glosses" (p. 39 and p. 169, respectively). But in Graff and Birkenstein's analysis of a published piece of text that directly follows (pp. 141–142), they highlighted phrases with other functions like "*it is my intention in this book*" and "*I must first explain,*" which seem closer to Vande Kopple's "commentary" function (p. 40), Williams's explanation of phrases that show "the writer's thinking and writing" (p. 66), or Hyland and Tse's "self-mentions" (p. 169). In addition, Graff and Birkenstein did not explain how those phrases clarify and elaborate—they simply said that the writer "stands apart from his main ideas" (p. 142). Furthermore, by having an entire chapter subtitled "*The Art of Metacommentary*" (p. 138), it would not be unreasonable for the casual reader to think that all of the metadiscourse moves would be discussed in this chapter. However, many of the classic metadiscourse moves appear in other chapters and are not labeled as such. For instance, they include a chapter titled "'As a Result': *Connecting the Parts*" (p. 107), which deals with what Vande Kopple terms "connectives" (p. 38), Williams names "logical connections" (p. 66), and Hyland and Tse call "transitions" (p. 169), but Graff and Birkenstein do not explicitly link this function to metadiscourse in the way that Williams, Vande Kopple, and Hyland and Tse do. Thus, Graff and Birkenstein's influential work, while it does introduce students to some of the metadiscourse functions and perhaps sets the stage for later explorations, does not contain the descriptions or explanations necessary for students to understand how metadiscourse works in different situations and how it affects the reading experience.

How Flow Is (or Is Not) Represented in Student-Facing Writing Resources

Frequently Used and Long-Standing Writing Instruction Texts

Many writing instructors assign readings from a writing instruction textbook and/or a handbook as part of the classroom experience. Student-facing writing texts come from a range of backgrounds: Some focus heavily on the process (e.g., Elbow's, 1998, *Writing With Power*) or on rhetorical concerns and audience (e.g., Rawlins & Metzger's, 2009, *The Writer's Way*); several focus on approaches influenced by cognitive schemas (e.g., Flower's multi-edition *Problem-Solving Strategies for Writers*); some take a research-focused approach (e.g., Booth et al.'s widely used *The Craft of Research*, 2016, in addition to earlier editions); and still others, like those by Williams and Vande Kopple, take an explicitly linguistic approach. Of course, there is a significant overlap across these approaches; for instance, *The Craft of Research*, being coauthored by Williams, naturally has some mention of linguistic principles (e.g., they mention the linguistic principle of old-before-new).

If the assigned textbook does not come from an author who explicitly considers linguistic principles, the discussion of flow is likely to be implicit at most and rely heavily on sensory terms describing problems for the reader: writing that is "choppy" (Rawlins & Metzger, 2009, p. 115), "disjointed" (Booth et al., 2016, p. 259), or moving in "fits and starts" as opposed to "smoothly" (Graff & Birkenstein, 2021, p. 109). Some suggestions for addressing the problems focus on transitions or connectors between sentences (Graff & Birkenstein; Rawlins & Metzger). Others suggest the use of repeated elements to increase cohesion, including repetition of key terms, repetition of key ideas, and "pointing words" (Graff & Birkenstein, 2021, p. 110), which could fit in with several of the rhetorical grammar models.

These pieces of advice are just that: pieces. They do not carry the systematic richness of the linguistics models that describe and explain connections in and across sentences or larger units of text. Without these more complete descriptions and explanations, pieces of advice that carry important suggestions may be overlooked if sentence-level changes are seen as meaningless editing. Writing instructors (in line with many writing textbooks) often make distinctions between revising for overall ideas and revising or editing sentences so that instruction begins with the higher level ideas and then focuses on sentence-level changes at the end of the writing process (Sommers, 2013), an approach well-supported by research in composition (e.g., Bereiter & Scardamalia, 1987; Fayol, 1999; Flower, 1979; Flower & Hayes, 1981; Kellogg, 2008). However, while many of these sentence-level changes that writing handbooks suggest might initially seem to be insignificant surface-level changes that do not influence the larger meaning of the writing, they almost certainly have an important effect on readers' perceptions of flow. Small changes may influence the reader's perception of sentence-to-sentence connections, the piece as a whole, and connections between a sentence and the text as a whole.

Metadiscourse is even less explicitly covered in writing textbooks than cohesion and coherence. Graff and Birkenstein's *They Say/I Say* is perhaps the most expansive on the topic. It presented templates that, among other things, do much of the work of metadiscourse and that on the surface align with the work of scholars in the field. These template phrases perform the two general functions that scholars have identified: one that signals the writer's attitude toward the propositional material and one that organizes and walks the reader through the material. However, it is doubtful to what extent this helps with flow, as Graff and Birkenstein are not very explicit about how these phrases organize the experience for the reader.

Popular Books on Style and Writing Handbooks

The issue of flow is also often not addressed in much detail in popular books on style or writing handbooks. None of the long-lasting popular books on style like Zinsser's (2010) *On Writing Well*, Fish's (2011) *How to Write a Sentence*, and Strunk and White's (2000) *The Elements of Style* mention flow, cohesion, or coherence but instead focus on ideas like avoiding passive voice, parallelism, and reducing nominalization. Handbooks, unlike books on style, focus heavily on issues of the writing process, academic writing style, common patterns of argument or analysis, citation, and correctness in usage. A quick glance at the stacks of back-issue writing handbooks that tend to accumulate in writing center tutoring sites shows that flow, cohesion, and coherence do not appear in the indexes of early common handbooks like *A Writer's Reference* (Hacker, 2007), *The St. Martin's Handbook* (Lunsford, 2011), or *The Everyday Writer* (Lunsford, 2013), as well as being absent in earlier editions of some of the textbooks described in the following paragraphs.

Later handbooks did sporadically mention flow in the index—always defined in terms of coherence (and not cohesion)—although the suggestions given for achieving flow included suggestions referencing what Williams would have termed elements contributing to both cohesion and coherence. For instance, Lunsford's (2019) *EasyWriter* mentioned flow in the index, but only if you looked for coherence first: "**coherence, 15** Also called 'flow,' the quality that makes a **text** seem unified" (p. 370, index). The discussion of flow also equated coherence and flow: "A paragraph has coherence—or flows—if its details fit together in a way that readers can easily follow" (p. 15). With respect to how to achieve coherence, what immediately followed were suggestions on organization ("general-to-specific"), "repetition of key words or phrases," "parallel structures," and "**transitions**" (p. 15), in ways that echo schema theories as well as certain aspects of what Williams would have called cohesion. Hacker and Sommer's *A Writer's Reference* (2021) followed this convention, explicitly equating flow with coherence in the index: "flow (coherence), **C**: 23–26" (p. 17 index) and offering the same standard ideas about "*linking ideas clearly*," "*repeating key words*," "*using parallel structures*," and "*providing transitions*" (pp. 23–26). Similarly, Glenn and Gray's (2017) *The Hodges Harbrace Handbook* didn't mention flow or cohesion but had entries under coherence, which discussed "unified and coherent" paragraphs (p. 361), again with the ideas of having a main idea, repeating elements, considering schemas within a paragraph, and using transitional phrases. Schwegler and Anson's (2014) *The Longman Handbook for Writers and Readers* took precisely the same approach. In common current handbooks, flow is defined in terms of coherence, but the suggestions for how to achieve coherence (or flow) are restricted to a strikingly small range of options.

Writing Handbook-Like Instruction on Writing Center Websites

Aside from writing instruction books, a primary source of advice for students comes from writing center websites. We briefly searched well-known writing center and program websites on July 7, 2023 for linked or embedded guidance on flow for students. In some cases, we did not find information on flow under the terms cohesion, coherence, or flow (see, e.g., the University of Michigan Sweetland Center for Writing, 2023, or the University of Chicago Writing Program, 2019—the same institution that Williams hailed from!). In other cases, searches did lead to specific references to flow but without additional information to help writers define, evaluate, or create flow. For example, a search might lead to a statement about tutors being able to help with flow, but nothing more. In general, while these sites conveyed that flow is important, they did not offer a means to address flow.

Other centers, however, did attempt to offer instruction on flow. However, a brief review of online writing center instructional manuals for students and teachers suggested considerable variability in how flow was discussed and how the terms cohesion and coherence were defined. This probably reflects the disciplinary background of the writer(s) or the works that they were familiar with. It may also reflect an attempt to cater to search terms that they think searchers will use, which again probably reflects different definitions available in texts that are still in use.

For instance, consider The Writing Center at the University of North Carolina at Chapel Hill's website. They maintain an extensive set of instructional materials aimed at undergraduate writers and have a handout titled *Flow*. Unlike many writing center or program handouts, theirs defined flow and linked it to both cohesion and coherence. They also explicitly cited a later version of Williams's *Ten Lessons in Style and Grace* (here, Williams and Bizup's *Style: Lessons in Clarity and Grace*, 2017), and their materials generally followed his distinctions between cohesion and coherence. The handout defined flow both in terms of sensory perceptions and how you achieve it:

> Writing that "flows" is easy to read smoothly from beginning to end. Readers don't have to stop, double back, reread, or work hard to find connections between ideas. Writers have structured the text so that it's clear and easy to follow. But how do you make your writing flow? Pay attention to coherence and cohesion.
> (The Writing Center at University of North Carolina at Chapel Hill, 2023, What is Flow? section)

This definition captures both the sensual and the metaphoric sense of flow, as well as organization and ideas. In the same entry, they further separated flow into "global" and "local" flow and mapped them, respectively, on definitions of coherence and cohesion, with coherence having to do with the logical order of ideas, and cohesion having to do with sentence-to-sentence connections (The Writing Center at the University of North Carolina at Chapel Hill, 2023, Coherence and Cohesion sections, respectively):

> Coherence, or global flow, means that ideas are sequenced logically at the higher levels: paragraphs, sections, and chapters. Readers can move easily from one major idea to the next without confusing jumps in the writer's train of thought. There's no single way to organize ideas, but there are common organizational patterns, including (but not limited to) . . .
>
> Cohesion, or local flow, means that the ideas are connected clearly at the sentence level. With clear connections between sentences, readers can move smoothly from one sentence to the next without stopping, doubling back, or trying to make sense of the text. Fortunately, writers can enhance cohesion with the following sentence-level strategies.

When discussing how to improve coherence, the authors described ways of looking at how ideas are sequenced, echoing Williams's approach and citing Williams and Bizup's (2017) *Style: Lessons in Clarity and Grace* (The

Writing Center at the University of North Carolina at Chapel Hill, 2023). When discussing cohesion, the authors mentioned several strategies, including transitional expressions, repeated elements through pronoun use, and "known-before-new" (also known as given-new), thus covering some uses of metadiscourse and some concepts from rhetorical grammar. Like *They Say/I Say*, the website suggestions are selective; they do not include complete taxonomies of metadiscourse or the systematic grammatical information underlying rhetorical grammar. However, they are very clear about treating global coherence as a matter of organization and progression of topics, and local cohesion as being a function of smaller sentence-level choices.

In contrast, consider the Purdue Online Writing Lab (OWL), which is somewhat less explicit about bringing concerns together and about the distinction between cohesion and coherence (more in line with Vande Kopple than with Williams). A search for flow on their website (July 7, 2023) found two handouts: *Flow in Scholarly Writing* and *Paragraph Organization and Flow* (a video with associated handout material), with both being found in sections of the website geared toward graduate students. The *Paragraph Organization and Flow* material (Purdue Online Writing Lab, 2022a) mentioned "major components of paragraph-level writing such as unity, coherence, and development" (para. 1) but, for the most part, referred back to *Flow in Scholarly Writing* for the bulk of the content (Campbell, 2016).

In *Flow in Scholarly Writing* (Campbell, 2016), the author defined flow generally as "how easily a reader can get into the text. . . . how easily the reader moves past the text and into a reading experience" but more concretely articulated the absence of flow with sensory descriptors like "choppy" or "disjointed" (para. 2). In the next sections, they further divided flow into two categories: "sentence level" and "paragraph level." On the sentence level, they indicated that "varied sentence structure" (para. 5) will contribute to flow. They also suggested a range of concerns relevant to readability and discourse community standards, as well as the connective function of metadiscourse. For paragraph-level flow, they discussed a generalized schema for developing paragraphs, including a topic sentence, a single idea, and supporting evidence. They then included something called "textual-level flow" (para. 7), which appears to describe the overall expectations of a generalized academic paper, including an introduction including a hypothesis or a question or a thesis, body paragraph, and a conclusion that reviews main conclusions and "other discipline-appropriate content" (para 7). Their definition of flow in this handout seems to largely rely on organization, structure, and discourse community concerns.

A search on the Purdue OWL website (July 7, 2023) for cohesion and coherence revealed a considerable overlap in how they were using the terms—more in line with early Vande Kopple than Williams, although all handouts cited Williams (and not Vande Kopple). A search for "cohesion" turned up three handouts: *Revising for Cohesion* and *Paragraph Organization & Flow* (doing a general Google search added the *On Paragraphs* handout). Notably, a search for the term "coherence" turned up the same three handouts, suggesting a considerable overlap in the terms the search engine is using. *Paragraph Organization & Flow* was the graduate-targeted material described previously. *Revising for Cohesion* and *On Paragraphs* were targeted at the undergraduate population.

Revising for Cohesion (Purdue Online Writing Lab, 2022b) stated at the top that it, like other online sites, was adapted from Williams's *Style: Ten Lessons in Clarity and Grace* (edition not specified). The major focus was on topic progression—but in a way that Williams (2003) himself relates to coherence (not cohesion!). In contrast, in the *On Paragraphs* (Purdue Online Writing Lab, 2022c) handout, the authors focused on ritualized determinants of paragraph structure and coherence:

> To be as effective as possible, a paragraph should contain each of the following: **Unity, Coherence, A Topic Sentence,** and **Adequate Development**. As you will see, all of these traits overlap. Using and adapting them to your individual purposes will help you construct effective paragraphs.
>
> (Elements of a Paragraph section)

In the same section, they went on to describe coherence this way: "Coherence is the trait that makes the paragraph easily understandable to a reader. You can help create coherence in your paragraphs by creating logical bridges and verbal bridges." In their descriptions of logical bridges (Logical Bridges section), they explained again that a "topic is carried over from sentence to sentence" (in line with Williams), and in the description of verbal bridges (Verbal Bridges section), they listed both concepts relevant to cohesion, as described by Williams (e.g., repetition of key words and synonyms), and metadiscourse (e.g., "transition words").

Taking all three handouts together, it is clear that the Purdue OWL site is using a significantly less consistent framework for describing cohesion and coherence than the University of North Carolina at Chapel Hill's and that their conceptions of flow rest heavily on overall organization and discourse community concerns. A comparison of the two entries aimed at undergraduates that contain material about cohesion and coherence suggests that they are both focusing on the importance of topic progressions but calling them, respectively, cohesion and coherence. The handout on cohesion did not contain information on most of the ways that sentence-to-sentence connections can be made; this was instead limited to the handout on paragraphs, which students may not understand is related to cohesion. In contrast, the flow materials aimed at the graduate students quite reasonably focused on concerns of discourse community expectations but neglected cohesion and coherence.

Graduate-Level Writing Textbooks

A review of writing instruction books aimed at graduate-level writing shows that—just like undergraduate writing resources—some focus on broad rhetorical concepts related to flow such as unity, organization, and a well-developed idea, whereas others discuss rhetorical choices at the sentence level in ways that probably reflect disciplinary expectations. Writing handbooks explicitly aimed at the humanities (e.g., *Professional Academic Writing in the Humanities and Social Sciences*, MacDonald, 1994; *The Elements of Academic Style: Writing for the Humanities*, Hayot, 2014) did not seem to mention flow, cohesion, or coherence explicitly, although they did mention the idea of an argument holding together. This limited attention to flow probably harks back to the idea that through the writing process, the writer will naturally create a well-formed argument that flows.

However, Swales and Feak's popular *Academic Writing for Graduate Students* (2012) referred explicitly to flow, as well as logical connectors and given-new. This book, a staple of early graduate writing classes in many disciplines, is more focused on social, natural, and applied sciences than humanities. Similarly, a quick review of widely used books or articles targeted at scientific writing shows that they addressed questions of flow, both in terms of cognitive schema (appropriately targeted toward the discipline or situation) and in terms of explicit linguistic concepts. Hofmann's (2010, and later editions) *Scientific Writing and Communication: Papers, Proposals, and Presentations* went even further. It mentioned flow explicitly, as well as coordination of ideas, parallel construction, paragraph coherence, and cohesion and word location, with an explicit mention of how small sentence-level changes can influence flow: "When authors arrange sentences to be cohesive, they consider word location. Good word location creates good 'flow' of a paragraph" (p. 113). This echoes some of the principles from Halliday and Hasan (1976) and emphasizes that flow can be enacted, in part, by seemingly small changes at the sentence level.

This focus on scientific writing may not be surprising. As noted earlier, Gopen and Swan (1990) long ago published an article in *American Scientist* on improving scientific writing by using given-new and end-focus to make sentence-level revisions, suggesting that scientists were starting even at this point to think about readability. It is also worth considering that the analytical nature of this linguistics-based approach might align well with scientific thinking.

What Does This Mean for Students?

Regardless of the reference textbook or materials used, if the student does not have instruction in a linguistically influenced way of writing, they generally rely on the ear as part of a voice-based approach. While this approach is widely accepted by students and instructors for finding flow issues, using it to address flow issues is more complicated. In *Vernacular Eloquence*, a book targeted at instructors and not students, Elbow suggested a trial-and-error approach:

> Sometimes it's enough to grab and shake myself, as it were, and demand a solution. . . . This can work. But plenty of times it doesn't. My search for a solution is often more like solving an intellectual puzzle: *What are some ways I could rearrange these words and find others and still say what I want to say?* I have to start fiddling with the words in a brute random way. *What if I started with the final phrase? What different words could I use?* It's often a process of trial and error.
>
> (Elbow, 2012, p. 229)

However, as he himself hinted, this isn't easy. In addition, as Bleich (1998) noted, this approach can itself be fraught with difficulties as both students and instructors develop ears for what norms in the field sound like (or what they think they sound like), which may not actually reflect concerns of flow or readability. Indeed, Elbow himself seems to recognize this issue; in *Vernacular Eloquence*, he made reference to the rhetorical grammar principle of given-new (p. 96) as one way of looking at flow, suggesting that additional approaches can be helpful in resolving issues.

If the instructor is not using one of these linguistically inflected textbooks, the absence of tools for addressing flow leaves writers who do not sense the issues or know how to address them with very little support. As Lancaster (2012) said, "if instructors do not enable students to make decisions about textual 'flow' by providing them with linguistic criteria for making those decisions, then merely sending students out to reformulate and recombine sentences may give rise to other textual problems" (p. 99).

This need for analytical approaches beyond recognizing and diagnosing using ear-based approaches seems especially relevant in today's writing pedagogy world, which is increasingly focusing on concerns of equity and inclusion (Shapiro, 2020) and giving students as many different ways as possible to master the material (Wiggins & McTighe, 2005). Our students come from a range of linguistic traditions. Increasingly, students in our classrooms—and their instructors—speak first languages other than English, which may influence their sense of flow on multiple levels. Furthermore, we realize that even the term *English* is problematic and should be treated as *Englishes*—increasingly, inhabitants of places where English is spoken hear multiple different variants of English (Canagarajah, 2006; Hall, 2018; Matsuda & Tardy, 2007). This complicates the issue of assessing flow and revising in at least two ways: Listeners are becoming more inured to subtle disruptions in their expected sense of the language or are willing to put in the increased cognitive effort to make meaning, and writers/speakers may have different senses of what works than the readers/listeners do. Furthermore, it is also worth noting that some of our students, especially members of the Deaf community, may not have access to ear-based approaches (Gonzales & Butler, 2020; Meranda, 2020).

Herding cats is not easy. But the literature review does point to some convergences. It suggests that readers' perceptions of flow are related to both cohesion and coherence (despite some differences in how cohesion and coherence are defined) and that there are a range of textual choices for enacting these concepts. This review also suggests that flow is influenced by the macro-level choices related to ideas and organization, harking back to ancient rhetoric's idea of *unity*, as well as the micro-level choices that set up sentence-to-sentence connections, connections within paragraphs, and sometimes even organization across the entire work. At the sentence and phrase levels, writers have a multitude of choices that send signals about how parts are related in ways both subtle and direct, and these choices almost certainly attend to concerns related to flow as well as other concerns.

While the cats are not of a single herd, they are circling around the same territory. And we may be able to corral them further using a multidisciplinary approach. It is clear that readers and writers have strong implicit and subjective views on flow and that they respond to the flow of writing. However, unless teachers and students use linguistic knowledge of flow in writing—and sometimes even then, depending on what sources they use—the term *flow* remains at once shared and ill-defined, making it especially difficult to teach without a multidisciplinary approach.

Put differently, the varied and, at times, vague perspectives on flow suggest that it is a rich and complex concept that requires a definition that brings together multiple perspectives and multiple disciplines. In this literature review, we have aimed to bring these different perspectives, these different voices, into a single conversation. In each of the following chapters, we add to this conversation the voices of students, instructors, and this study's researchers in order to enrich our understanding of flow in ways that benefit writers and writing instruction.

Notes

1. First published in 1981, this book has been reprinted under different titles, sometimes known as *Style: Lessons in Clarity and Grace*, or, in its incarnation for professionals, *Style: Toward Clarity and Grace*.
2. This text was originally published in 1994. Here we are working from the 4th edition published in 2013.

References

Aristotle. (1994). *Poetics* (S. H. Butcher, Trans.). The Internet Classics Archive. http://classics.mit.edu/Aristotle/poetics.1.1.html (Original work published ca. 350 B.C.E.)

Aull, L. (2015a). *First-year university writing: A corpus-based study with implications for pedagogy*. Palgrave Macmillan.
Aull, L. (2015b). Linguistic attention in rhetorical genre studies and first year writing. *Composition Forum, 31*. https://compositionforum.com/issue/31/linguistic-attention.php
Aull, L. (2019). Linguistic markers of stance and genre in upper-level student writing. *Written Communication, 36*(2), 267–295. https://doi.org/10.1177/0741088318819
Aull, L. (2021). What is "good writing?" Analyzing metadiscourse as civil discourse. *Journal of Teaching Writing, 36*(1), 37–60. https://journals.iupui.edu/index.php/teachingwriting/article/view/26240
Aull, L. L., & Lancaster, Z. (2014). Linguistic markers of stance in early and advanced academic writing: A corpus-based comparison. *Written Communication, 31*(2), 151–183. https://doi.org/10.1177/0741088314527055
Austin, J. L. (1975). *How to do things with words* (M. Sbisà & J. O. Urmson, Eds.; 2nd ed.). Harvard University Press.
Bakhtin, M. M. (1981). *The dialogic imagination: Four essays* (M. Holquist, Ed. & Trans., C. Emerson, Trans.). University of Texas Press.
Barron, A., Gu, Y., & Steen, G. (Eds.). (2017). Pragmatics broadly viewed. In *The Routledge handbook of pragmatics* (pp. 1–3). Routledge. https://doi.org/10.4324/9781315668925
Beaufort, A. (2007). *College writing and beyond: A new framework for university writing instruction*. Utah State University Press.
Beaver, D. I., Roberts, C., Simons, M., & Tonhauser, J. (2017). Questions under discussion: Where information structure meets projective content. *Annual Review of Linguistics, 3*, 265–284. https://doi.org/10.1146/annurev-linguistics-011516-033952
Bereiter, C., & Scardamalia, M. (1987). *The psychology of written composition*. L. Erlbaum Associates.
Bizzell, P. (1992). What is a discourse community? In *Academic discourse and critical consciousness* (pp. 222–237). University of Pittsburgh Press. https://doi.org/10.2307/j.ctt7zwb7k.14
Bleich, D. (1998). *Know and tell: A writing pedagogy of disclosure, genre, and membership*. Boynton/Cook Publishers.
Booth, W. C., Colomb, G. G., Williams, J. M., Bizup, J., & FitzGerald, W. T. (2016). *The craft of research* (4th ed.). University of Chicago Press.
Booth, W. C., & Gregory, M. W. (1987). *The Harper and Row rhetoric: Writing as thinking, thinking as writing*. Harper & Row.
Burke, K. (1969). *A rhetoric of motives*. University of California Press.
Burke, K. (1974). *The philosophy of literary form*. University of California Press.
Campbell, M. M. (2016). *Flow in scholarly writing*. Purdue University Writing Lab. https://owl.purdue.edu/owl/graduate_writing/documents/Flow-Handout.pdf
Canagarajah, A. S. (2006, June). The place of world Englishes in composition: Pluralization continued. *College Composition and Communication, 57*(4), 586–619.
Chafe, W. (1994). *Discourse, consciousness, and time: The flow and displacement of conscious experience in speaking and writing*. University of Chicago Press.

Chaplin, M. T. (1984). Foreword. In R. B. Markels (Eds.), *A new perspective on cohesion in expository paragraphs* (pp. vii–ix). Southern Illinois University Press.
Csikszentmihalyi, M. (1990). *Flow: The psychology of optimal experience* (1st ed.). Harper & Row.
Devitt, A. J. (2004). A proposal for teaching genre awareness and antecedent genres. In *Writing genres* (pp. 191–213). Southern Illinois University Press.
Dictionary.com. (n.d.). Cohesion. *Dictionary.com Dictionary*. Retrieved July 7, 2023, from www.dictionary.com/browse/cohesion
Duncan, M. (2007). Whatever happened to the paragraph? *College English, 69*(5), 470–495.
Ede, L., & Lunsford, A. (1984). Audience addressed/audience invoked: The role of audience in composition theory and pedagogy. *College Composition and Communication, 35*(2), 155–171. https://doi.org/10.2307/358093
Elbow, P. (1998a). *Writing with power: Techniques for mastering the writing process* (2nd ed.). Oxford University Press.
Elbow, P. (1998b). *Writing without teachers* (2nd ed.). Oxford University Press.
Elbow, P. (2012). *Vernacular eloquence: What speech can bring to writing*. Oxford University Press.
Elbow, P., & Belanoff, P. (1989). *A community of writers: A workshop course in writing* (1st ed.). Random House.
Elbow, P., & Belanoff, P. (2000). *Sharing and responding* (3rd ed.). McGraw-Hill Higher Education.
Emig, J. (1983). *The web of meaning: Essays on writing, teaching, learning, and thinking* (D. Goswami & M. Butler, Eds.). Boynton/Cook Publishers.
Fayol, M. (1999). From on-line management problems to strategies in written composition. In M. Torrance & G. C. Jeffery (Eds.), *The cognitive demands of writing: Processing capacity and working memory effects in text production*. Amsterdam University Press.
Fish, S. (2011). *How to write a sentence: And how to read one*. HarperCollins.
Fitzgerald, J. (1995). English-as-a-second-language learners' cognitive reading processes: A review of research in the United States. *Review of Educational Research, 65*(2), 145–190. https://doi.org/10.2307/1170711
Flower, L. (1979). Writer-based prose: A cognitive basis for problems in writing. *College English, 41*(1), 19–37. https://doi.org/10.2307/376257
Flower, L. (1993). *Problem-solving strategies for writing* (4th ed.). Harcourt Brace Jovanovich College Publishers.
Flower, L., & Hayes, J. R. (1980). The cognition of discovery: Defining a rhetorical problem. *College Composition and Communication, 31*(1), 21–32. https://doi.org/10.2307/356630
Flower, L., & Hayes, J. R. (1981). A cognitive process theory of writing. *College Composition and Communication, 32*(4), 365–387. https://doi.org/10.2307/356600
Glenn, C., & Gray, L. (2017). *The Hodges Harbrace handbook* (19th ed.). Cengage Learning.
Gonzales, L., & Butler, J. (2020). Working toward social justice through multilingualism, multimodality, and accessibility in writing classrooms.

Composition Forum, 44. https://compositionforum.com/issue/44/multilingualism.php

Gopen, G. D., & Swan, J. A. (1990). The science of scientific writing. *American Scientist, 78*(6), 550–558.

Graff, G., & Birkenstein, C. (2010). *They say/I say: The moves that matter in academic writing* (2nd ed.). W. W. Norton & Company.

Graff, G., & Birkenstein, C. (2021). *They say/I say: The moves that matter in academic writing* (5th ed.). W. W. Norton & Company.

Grice, P. (1989). *Studies in the way of words.* Harvard University Press. https://hdl.handle.net/2027/heb08428.0001.001

Hacker, D. (2007). *A writer's reference* (6th ed.). Bedford/St. Martin's.

Hacker, D., & Sommers, N. (2021). *A writer's reference* (10th ed.). Bedford/St. Martin's.

Hall, J. (2018). The translingual challenge: Boundary work in rhetoric & composition, second language writing, and WAC/WID. *Across the Disciplines, 15*(3), 28–47. https://doi.org/10.37514/ATD-J.2018.15.3.10

Halliday, M. A. K., & Hasan, R. (1976). *Cohesion in English.* Longman.

Halliday, M. A. K., & Martin, J. R. (1993). *Writing science: Literacy and discursive power.* Routledge. https://doi-org/10.4324/9780203209936

Halliday, M. A. K., & Matthiessen, C. M. (2013). *Halliday's introduction to functional grammar* (4th ed.). Routledge. https://doi-org/10.4324/9780203431269

Hancock, C. (2005). *Meaning-centered grammar: An introductory text.* Equinox.

Harris, J. (2006). *Rewriting: How to do things with texts.* Utah State University Press.

Hartwell, P. (1979). Teaching arrangement: A pedagogy. *College English, 40*(5), 548–554. https://doi.org/10.2307/376327

Hayot, E. (2014). *The elements of academic style: Writing for the humanities.* Columbia University Press.

Hofmann, A. H. (2010). *Scientific writing and communication: Papers, proposals, and presentations.* Oxford University Press.

Hyland, K. (1999). Disciplinary discourses: Writer stance in research articles. In C. N. Candlin & K. Hyland (Eds.), *Writing: Texts, processes and practices* (1st ed., pp. 99–121). Routledge. https://doi.org/10.4324/9781315840390

Hyland, K. (2003). Genre-based pedagogies: A social response to process. *Journal of Second Language Writing, 12*(1), 17–29. https://doi.org/10.1016/S1060-3743(02)00124-8

Hyland, K. (2005). Stance and engagement: A model of interaction in academic discourse. *Discourse Studies, 7*(2), 173–192. https://doi.org/10.1177/1461445605050365

Hyland, K. (2007). Genre pedagogy: Language, literacy and L2 writing instruction. *Journal of Second Language Writing, 16*(3), 148–164. https://doi.org/10.1016/j.jslw.2007.07.005

Hyland, K. (2008). Genre and academic writing in the disciplines. *Language Teaching, 41*(4), 543–562. https://doi.org/10.1017/S0261444808005235

Hyland, K. (2011). Disciplines and discourses: Social interactions in the construction of knowledge. In D. Starke-Meyerring, A. Paré, N. Artemeva, M.

Horne, & L. Yousoubova (Eds.), *Writing in knowledge societies* (pp. 193–214). The WAC Clearinghouse; Parlor Press. https://doi.org/10.37514/PER-B.2011.2379.2.10

Hyland, K., & Tse, P. (2004). Metadiscourse in academic writing: A reappraisal. *Applied Linguistics, 25*(2), 156–177. https://doi.org/10.1093/applin/25.2.156

Johns, A. M. (1986). The ESL student and the revision process: Some insights from schema theory. *Journal of Basic Writing, 5*(2), 70–80.

Johns, A. M. (1997). *Text, role, and context: Developing academic literacies.* Cambridge University Press.

Kehler, A., & Rohde, H. (2017). Evaluating an expectation-driven question-under-discussion model of discourse interpretation. *Discourse Processes, 54*(3), 219–238. https://doi.org/10.1080/0163853X.2016.1169069

Kellogg, R. T. (2008). Training writing skills: A cognitive developmental perspective. *Journal of Writing Research, 1*(1), 1–26. https://doi.org/10.17239/jowr-2008.01.01.1

Knoblauch, C. H., & Brannon, L. (1984). *Rhetorical traditions and the teaching of writing.* Boynton/Cook Publishers.

Kolln, M., & Gray, L. (2017). *Rhetorical grammar: Grammatical choices, rhetorical effects.* Pearson.

Kuriloff, P. C. (1996). What discourses have in common: Teaching the transaction between writer and reader. *College Composition and Communication, 47*(4), 485–501. https://doi.org/10.2307/358598

Lancaster, C. I. (2012). *Stance and reader positioning in upper-level student writing in political theory and economics.* [Doctoral dissertation, University of Michigan]. Deep Blue Documents. https://deepblue.lib.umich.edu/handle/2027.42/93976

Lancaster, Z. (2014). Exploring valued patterns of stance in upper-level student writing in the disciplines. *Written Communication, 31*(1), 27–57. https://doi.org/10.1177/0741088313515170

Lancaster, Z. (2016a). Do academics really write this way? A corpus investigation of moves and templates in "They say/I say". *College Composition and Communication, 67*(3), 437–464.

Lancaster, Z. (2016b). Expressing stance in undergraduate writing: Discipline-specific and general qualities. *Journal of English for Academic Purposes, 23*, 16–30. https://doi.org/10.1016/j.jeap.2016.05.006

Larsson, S. (1996). *Computing implicature: The case of relevance* [Master's thesis, University of Göteborg]. https://citeseerx.ist.psu.edu/viewdoc/download?doi=10.1.1.592.6349&rep=rep1&type=pdf

Leahy, R. (1995). When the going is good: Implications of "flow" and "liking" for writers and tutors. *The Writing Center Journal, 15*(2), 152–162.

LeCluyse, C. (2013). The categories we keep: Writing center forms and the *topoi* of writing. *Praxis: A Writing Center Journal, 10*(2), 1–9. https://repositories.lib.utexas.edu/handle/2152/62176

Leki, I. (1991). Twenty-five years of contrastive rhetoric: Text analysis and writing pedagogies. *TESOL Quarterly, 25*(1), 123–143. https://doi.org/10.2307/3587031

Lunsford, A. A. (2011). *The St. Martin's handbook* (7th ed.). Bedford/St. Martin's.

Lunsford, A. A. (2013). *The everyday writer: Instructor's edition* (5th ed.). Bedford/St. Martin's.

Lunsford, A. A. (2019). *EasyWriter* (7th ed.). Bedford/St. Martin's.

Lunsford, A. A., & Ede, L. S. (1984). Classical rhetoric, modern rhetoric, and contemporary discourse studies. *Written Communication, 1*(1), 78–100. https://doi.org/10.1177/0741088384001001004

MacDonald, S. P. (1994). *Professional academic writing in the humanities and social sciences*. Southern Illinois University Press.

Matsuda, P. K., & Tardy, C. M. (2007). Voice in academic writing: The rhetorical construction of author identity in blind manuscript review. *English for Specific Purposes, 26*(2), 235–249. https://doi.org/10.1016/j.esp.2006.10.001

Meranda, S. K. (2020). *Discerning consistent evidence-based communication strategies for supporting deaf writers in the first year composition classroom: A study*. [Master's thesis, Indiana University]. IUPUI ScholarWorks. https://scholarworks.iupui.edu/bitstream/handle/1805/23692/SMeranda_MA2020_ThesisSubmission_ScholarWorks.pdf?sequence=11

Micciche, L. R. (2004). Making a case for rhetorical grammar. *College Composition and Communication, 55*(4), 716–731. https://doi.org/10.2307/4140668

Miller, C. R. (1984). Genre as social action. *Quarterly Journal of Speech, 70*(2), 151–167. https://doi.org/10.1080/00335638409383686

Murray, D. M. (1985). *A writer teaches writing* (2nd ed.). Houghton Mifflin.

Murray, D. M. (2004). *The craft of revision* (5th ed.). Cengage Learning.

Myers, G. (1990). *Writing biology: Texts in the social construction of scientific knowledge*. The University of Wisconsin Press.

Newman, S. P. (1995). *A practical system of rhetoric, or the principles and rules of style* (C. Downey, Ed.). Scholars' Facsimiles & Reprints. (Original work published 1835)

North, S. (2005). Disciplinary variation in the use of theme in undergraduate essays. *Applied Linguistics, 26*(3), 431–452. https://doi.org/10.1093/applin/ami031

Oxford Learner's Dictionaries. (n.d.). Cohesion. *Oxford Learner's Dictionaries*. Retrieved February 21, 2021, from www.oxfordlearnersdictionaries.com/us/definition/english/cohesion

Paraskevas, C. C. (2021). *Exploring grammar through texts: Reading and writing the structure of English*. Routledge.

Podis, J. M., & Podis, L. A. (1990). Identifying and teaching rhetorical plans for arrangement. *College Composition and Communication, 41*(4), 430–442. https://doi.org/10.2307/357932

Purdue Online Writing Lab. (2022a). *Paragraph organization and flow*. https://owl.purdue.edu/owl/graduate_writing/thesis_and_dissertation/paragraph_organization_flow.html

Purdue Online Writing Lab. (2022b). *Revising for cohesion*. https://owl.purdue.edu/owl/general_writing/the_writing_process/proofreading/revising_for_cohesion.html

Purdue Online Writing Lab. (2022c). *On paragraphs*. https://owl.purdue.edu/owl/general_writing/academic_writing/paragraphs_and_paragraphing/index.html

Rawlins, J., & Metzger, S. (2009). *The writer's way* (7th ed.). Houghton Mifflin.
Raymond, L., & Quinn, Z. (2012). What a writer wants: Assessing fulfillment of student goals in writing center tutoring sessions. *The Writing Center Journal, 32*(1), 64–77.
Roberts, C. (2012). Information structure: Towards an integrated formal theory of pragmatics. *Semantics & Pragmatics, 5*, 1–69. https://doi.org/10.3765/sp.5.6
Rossen-Knill, D. F. (2011). Flow and the principle of relevance: Bringing our dynamic speaking knowledge to writing. *Journal of Teaching Writing, 26*(1), 39–67. https://journals.iupui.edu/index.php/teachingwriting/article/view/26270/24281
Rossen-Knill, D. F. (2013). Refining the given-new expectation for classroom use: A lesson in the importance of audience. *Journal of Teaching Writing, 28*(1), 21–51. https://journals.iupui.edu/index.php/teachingwriting/article/view/20717/20250
Salvatore, J. (2021). Tools, not rules: Rhetorical grammar as a meaning-making tool in the creative writing workshop. *Journal of Teaching Writing, 36*(1), 91–128. https://journals.iupui.edu/index.php/teachingwriting/article/view/26242/24359
Schultz, J. (1977). The story workshop method: Writing from start to finish. *College English, 39*(4), 411–436. https://doi.org/10.2307/375765
Schwegler, R. A., & Anson, C. M. (2014). *The Longman handbook for writers and readers* (6th ed.). Pearson.
Searle, J. R. (1969). *Speech acts: An essay in the philosophy of language.* Cambridge University Press.
Shapiro, S. (2020). Inclusive pedagogy in the academic writing classroom: Cultivating communities of belonging. *Journal of Academic Writing, 10*(1), 154–164. https://doi.org/10.18552/joaw.v10i1.607
Sommers, N. (2013). *Responding to student writers.* Bedford/St. Martin's.
Sperber, D., & Wilson, D. (1995). *Relevance: Communication and cognition* (2nd ed.). Blackwell Publishing.
Strunk, W., Jr., & White, E. B. (2000). *The elements of style* (4th ed.). Allyn & Bacon.
Swales, J. M. (1990). *Genre analysis: English in academic and research settings* (C. A. Chapelle & S. Hunston, Eds.). Cambridge University Press.
Swales, J. M. (2004). *Research genres: Explorations and applications* (M. H. Long & J. C. Richards, Eds.). Cambridge University Press.
Swales, J. M., & Feak, C. B. (2012). *Academic writing for graduate students: Essential tasks and skills* (3rd ed.). University of Michigan Press.
University of Chicago Writing Program. (2019). *University of Chicago.* https://writing-program.uchicago.edu
University of Michigan Sweetland Writing Center. (2023). *University of Michigan.* https://lsa.umich.edu/sweetland
Vande Kopple, W. J. (1985). Some exploratory discourse on metadiscourse. *College Composition and Communication, 36*(1), 82–93. https://doi.org/10.2307/357609

Vande Kopple, W. J. (1989). *Clear and coherent prose*. Scott, Foresman and Company.

Vande Kopple, W. J. (1991). Themes, thematic progressions, and some implications for understanding discourse. *Written Communication, 8*(3), 311–347. https://doi.org/10.1177/0741088391008003002

Vande Kopple, W. J. (2002). Metadiscourse, discourse, and issues in composition and rhetoric. In E. L. Barton & G. Stygall (Eds.), *Discourse studies in composition* (pp. 91–113). Hampton Press.

Vande Kopple, W. J. (2012). The importance of studying metadiscourse. *Applied Research on English Language, 1*(2), 37–44. https://doi.org/10.22108/ARE.2012.15453

Wardle, E. (2009). "Mutt genres" and the goal of FYC: Can we help students write the genres of the university? *College Composition and Communication, 60*(4), 765–789.

Wiggins, G., & McTighe, J. (2005). *Understanding by design* (expanded 2nd ed.). ASCD.

Williams, J. M. (1981). *Style: Ten lessons in clarity & grace*. Scott, Foresman and Company.

Williams, J. M. (2003). *Style: Ten lessons in clarity and grace* (7th ed.). Addison-Wesley Educational Publishers.

The Writing Center at the University of North Carolina at Chapel Hill. (2023). *Flow*. University of North Carolina at Chapel Hill. https://writingcenter.unc.edu/tips-and-tools/flow/

Zinsser, W. (2006). *On writing well* (7th ed. rev.). Collins.

2 What Do College Students Say?

In Chapter 1, we presented a range of perspectives on flow in writing from student-facing texts and the key scholarly works informing these texts. In this chapter, we turn to undergraduates themselves to learn their perspectives on flow prior to receiving instruction on flow in first-year writing courses. The students' perspectives are based on a preinstruction flow questionnaire designed as part of a larger study that investigated the efficacy of two approaches to teaching flow in writing: one based on voice and senses (Elbow, 2012; Elbow & Belanoff, 1989; Schultz, 1977) and the other that combines rhetorical grammar (Hancock, 2005; Kolln & Gray, 2017; Noguchi, 1991, 2002; Rossen-Knill, 2013; Vande Kopple, 1989; Williams, 2003) and the principle of relevance as adapted for writing instruction (Rossen-Knill, 2013; Rossen-Knill & Bakhmetyeva, 2011). The preinstruction flow questionnaire was administered to 166 students enrolled in first-year writing courses taught by 11 instructors from two private four-year colleges in the Northeastern United States. The questionnaire's purpose was to learn what elements students identified when they considered how to create flow in their own writing. Specifically, we asked,

1. What, if anything, do you typically do to determine if your own writing is flowing well?
2. When you learn that your writing doesn't flow, what do you do to try to fix it?
3. What techniques have you been taught to improve the flow of your writing?

We coded students' responses following a grounded theory approach (Corbin & Strauss, 1990; Saldaña, 2009). The multidisciplinary coding team included three faculty and two undergraduate writing tutors. While all team members worked in the Writing, Speaking, and Argument Program at the University of Rochester, disciplinary backgrounds spanned the natural sciences, social sciences, and humanities. Faculty members' PhDs are in English, English with a concentration in linguistics, and biology. One undergraduate coder was majoring in English and biology, the other in English and business.

The coding team read and discussed Corbin and Strauss (1990) and Saldaña (2009) to develop a shared understanding of the coding process and then began open coding with the first collected set of preinstruction questionnaire responses. Each team member independently marked anything that struck them as being related to the research questions on flow in writing, as well as anything that stood out for any reason at all. Coders maintained personal memos on responses to the data and shared and discussed with the team what struck them in students' responses to the questionnaire. As patterns emerged across quotations, team members labeled these patterns to create codes. Additionally, coders captured infrequent but especially interesting quotations with a code labeled *Juicy*. The team then began the process of applying the codes to the first and subsequent data sets in an order that followed the order of data collection. The team coded using a cyclic process of revising and refining the set of codes, a process that spanned approximately 16 months (October 2017 to February 2019) and led to robust conversations and 25 iterations of the codebook (available on request). The coding process reflected our emphasis on considering any and all perspectives on the data, as well as a commitment to hearing perspectives from all members of our multidisciplinary student–faculty team. Team members were invited to and regularly did challenge previous codes and suggest new ones. Throughout the coding process, codes were added, deleted, subsumed by one or more other codes, or refined for the purposes of clarification.

Codes were deleted from the codebook when they were extremely rare, as with *Goal*, "anything that seems like it relates to a goal": it was added to codebook 15 but later removed from codebook 17. However, if any team member expressed concern that removing a code resulted in salient quotations remaining uncoded, we captured these under the code *Juicy*. Codes were also taken out of the codebook when after coding several sets of data and after several attempts to refine the code, team members could not agree on the meaning of the code or reliably identify similar sets of quotations that would correspond to the code. For example, codebook 6 included the code *Collaborative*, which corresponded to "specifically names sharing work with others. Shared meaning-making process. Draws on reader to solve writing problem, but writer remains involved." The codebook example for *Collaborative* stated, "I read aloud to myself or to another person to see if writing is flowing well." As documented in our coding memos, the team questioned whether or not this differed enough from the code *Reading Aloud to Others* and had trouble reliably distinguishing between the two codes. Thus, *Collaborative* was removed but captured by *Reading Aloud to Others*.

Codes also evolved because some quotations were consistently double-coded across the same set of codes. While we allowed double-coding, consistent coding across the same set of categories led us to consider the possibility that related codes were not sufficiently distinct and thus might be reduced to one code. For example, because quotations coded as *Punctuation* were also regularly coded as *Small Text Unit*, the team decided to take *Punctuation* out of the codebook and instead code quotations that would have fallen under *Punctuation* as *Small Text Unit*. In this case, the team made the decision relatively quickly and easily.

In other cases, the team believed that overlapping codes captured important and different concepts and struggled with how to represent and distinguish codes. We especially struggled to find the boundary between the codes *Organization* and *Idea*, as the following brief narrative illustrates. In the first codebook, *Organizing Ideas* represented quotations that discussed organization and ideas as interdependent concepts: "Any discussion or description of how information or ideas are organized in the text: could be at the paragraph or essay level." Across the next few versions of the codebooks, based on the reasoning that one organizes something, *Organizing Ideas* was eventually shortened to *Organizing* and characterized as follows in codebook 4: "Any discussion or description of organizing ideas, thoughts, themes, logic, argument." Additionally, the codebook allowed for the possibility that ideas might be the focus of the quotation on organization and included relevant language: "When IDEAS are the focus, might include grouping, reordering, overall structure, outline, thesis as organizer. Also includes reference to connecting ideas because they are related or because of logical progression." A typical example for *Organizing*, which might reference the whole essay or a part of a sentence, is as follows: "Create insightful sentences that connect two ideas; find a common theme among them and then relate or contrast them" (codebook 5). An additional concern involved the potential overlap between *Organizing* and the code *Changing Text*. The code *Changing Text* involved the movements of text, and moving text affects organization. We ultimately determined that in *Changing Text*, the movement, not the organization, was the focus. Prototypical examples included "to take out the passive voice" and "I try to rewrite sentences, to try to restructure them" (codebook 5). We resolved this potential overlap in codebook 7, where we changed the code name *Organizing* back to *Organizing Ideas* to better capture the interrelatedness of organization and ideas in quotations. Thus, *Changing Text* remained with a focus on change rather than on the ordering of and relationships among ideas. However, overlap problems persisted. The team observed that the codebook failed to represent quotations about improving flow that were motivated by ideas and did not mention organization of textual elements, such as "Also reading it aloud helps me see if the ideas and sentences make sense" (codebook 8). This led to the addition of the code *Ideas* to codebook 8: "Mention or discussion of ideas as the basis for flow or revision. This is NOT about organizing those ideas—that goes under OI."

Over the next several coding sessions, team members coded using *Organizing Ideas* and *Ideas* and confirmed, on the one hand, that there remained an interrelatedness between them, and on the other hand, that there was a difference between a quotation that privileged ordering and a quotation that privileged ideas. This led to the decision, in codebook 12, to again change the name of the code *Organizing Ideas* to *Organization*, which is described as "organization (without explicitly referencing ideas). Any discussion or description of the organization, order, mapping, sequencing, etc." and "typical words: grouping, reordering, overall structure, outline, thesis as organizer." The team revised this definition to better emphasize the concept of ordering text: "To count as 'Organization' . . . explicit reference must be made to reordering/rearranging the sentence or sentences. Typical words: grouping, reordering, sequence, outline" (codebook 25). *Organization* might or might not include reference to ideas; the defining characteristic was the explicit reference to ordering text. Representative quotations follow, with the components that explicitly mention the ordering of text underlined: "<u>build up to</u> a main idea" and "<u>Having good organization</u> and clear claims" (codebook 25).

As a counterpoint to *Organization*, the code *Idea* emphasized the privileged place of ideas over the ordering of text: "Mention or discussion of ideas as the basis for flow or revision. Might involve 'coherence,' 'make sense,' 'unity,' 'theme,' and 'logic'" (codebook 25). The team also considered vocabulary that potentially referenced both a sense of ordering text and the idea of the text. In this regard, the word "connect" received special mention in the final codebook under the definition of *Idea* to help coders determine its meaning(s) in quotations:

> If "connect" seems to be used to refer to transitions between sentences or paragraphs, then we are not coding it as "I" [*Ideas*]. If "connect" seems to refer to ideas—even though some equivalent of "idea" is not explicitly mentioned—then we code it as "I."
>
> (codebook 25)

Representative quotations follow, with the components that reference the privileged place of ideas underlined:

1. Build up to a <u>main idea</u>
2. Having good organization and <u>clear claims</u>
3. Also reading it aloud helps me see <u>if the ideas and sentences make sense</u>
4. Create insightful sentences that connect <u>two ideas; find a common theme among them and then relate or contrast them</u>

As the evolution of the codes *Organization* and *Idea* makes clear, these concepts are intimately related—"connected" even at the level of vocabulary. At the same time, the coders' experiences with the data suggest that they are not the same, as evidenced by some quotations that seemed to be related either to the code *Organization* or *Idea*, but not both. For example, in the final data set, "I try to rewrite sentences, to try to restructure them" was coded only as *Organization* (as well as *Small Text Unit*), whereas "I first make sure my idea is getting across" was coded only as *Idea*. As a result, the team settled on two closely related but separate codes. As might be expected, however, many quotations had one part coded as *Organization* and another part coded as *Idea*, and in some cases, full quotations were double-coded as both *Organization* and *Idea*, as with "I make sure ideas are in a logical order, building up and interchanging toward a goal topic idea." The reasoning (and feeling) here was that it was impossible to reliably separate those elements captured by *Organization* from those captured by *Idea*. Trying to do so, the team concluded, would lead to misrepresenting the quotation's meaning.

Once we had established the final codebook, the coding team divided work so that all of the data were coded individually by rotating two-coder teams. Each team compared their coding results, discussed discrepancies, and settled straightforward discrepancies (e.g., someone misread a quotation or overlooked a quotation that had an obvious code). Other discrepancies were brought to the full coding team for discussion and to determine how to move forward. The final codebook included 17 codes.

For this book, we focused on five of the 17 codes because they capture especially well students' perceptions of the elements that account for flow in writing. Two of the most frequent codes correspond to relatively concrete aspects of an essay: *Small Text Unit* (28.68%) and *Organization* (9.82%). *Small Text Unit* involves "any mention of text at or below the sentence level (e.g., sentence, clause, phrase, words)," of a "sentence-level phenomenon or issue," or of "punctuation" (codebook 25). *Organization* is defined as, "any discussion or description of the organization, order, mapping, sequencing, etc. To count as 'Organization' within a sentence, explicit reference must be made to reordering/rearranging the sentence or sentences" (codebook 25).

The remaining three codes, *Idea*, *Sensory*, and *Audience Awareness*, relate to the high-order concerns of textual meaning and feeling from either a writer's or reader's perspective. The code *Idea* (19.12%) occurred frequently, whereas the codes *Sensory* (3.85%) and *Audience Awareness* (2.39%) occurred less frequently. *Idea* is defined as the "mention or discussion of ideas as the basis for flow or revision" (codebook 25). *Sensory* and *Audience Awareness* refer, respectively, to the representation of the writer's and the reader's respective experiences of the text. *Sensory* captures the writer's experience of their text and is defined as "focused description of experiencing a written paper (as opposed to using sense to produce a paper) in a sensory way, where the primary purpose of the excerpt is to describe how the writer is experiencing their work through senses" (codebook 25). *Audience Awareness* captures the writer's concern for a reader's experience and is defined as "actions or comments that suggest that writer has a particular interest in understanding the reader's perspective" (codebook 25).

In this book, we do not discuss the remaining 12 codes because they do not address our immediate concern for identifying the elements of flow in writing. Rather, they focus on students' descriptions of their strategies (or lack thereof) for evaluating flow, or they involve particular strategies for creating flow that we introduced as part of our larger study of flow in writing. More specifically, seven of the 12 codes focus on the particular strategies the writer used to review their own work (e.g., reading silently to oneself, reading aloud to an unspecified audience, and the reader reading aloud to the writer) as opposed to a focus on revising in response to the writer's or reader's perception of the text; four referred to revision strategies related to rhetorical grammar (e.g., given-new, end-focus, and principle of relevance); one corresponded to quotations that indicated that a student had little to no instruction in strategies related to flow.

Once all quotations were coded using the final codebook, two members of the coding team (a faculty member and a student) further analyzed quotations that corresponded to the five selected codes in order to deepen the understanding of how students represented elements of flow. As the following discussion illustrates, students' responses revealed a high degree of consistency in how they talked about flow, as well as some interesting variation. It is worth noting that the students' comments point to many of the same elements raised by scholars. That said, students' comments also suggest the need for a deeper, more explicit understanding of flow, as well as the need for a consistent and flexible definition that is grounded in writing as a rhetorical act.

The next section focuses on the five selected codes—*Idea, Organization, Sensory, Audience Awareness,* and *Small Text Unit*—and, more specifically, the corresponding students' comments on flow in writing. Table 2.1 provides an overview of key definitions.

Table 2.1 Codes Representing Students' Perspectives on Flow

Code	Brief Definition	Example
Idea	Mention or discussion of ideas as the basis for flow or revision.	"Create insightful sentences that connect two ideas; find a common theme among them and then relate or contrast them"
Organization	Organization (without explicitly referencing ideas). Any discussion or description of the organization, order, mapping, sequencing, etc. To count as "Organization" within a sentence, explicit reference must be made to reordering/rearranging the sentence or sentences.	"I make sure ideas are in a logical order, building up and interchanging toward a goal topic idea"
Sensory	Focused description of experiencing a written paper (as opposed to using sense to produce a paper) in a sensory way, where the primary purpose of the excerpt is to describe how the writer is experiencing their work through senses.	"I read whatever I'm writing out loud so I can hear the rhythm of my work"

Table 2.1 (Continued)

Code	Brief Definition	Example
Audience Awareness	Actions or comments that suggest that the writer has a particular interest in understanding the reader's perspective.	"Once reading my essay over I determine if I believe if the reader can understand my point"
Small Text Unit	Any mention of text at or below the sentence level (e.g., sentence, clause, phrase, and words). Any mention of a sentence-level phenomenon or issue. Includes moving a sentence. Includes mention of punctuation.	"I've learned to use different words in my vocabulary, to not have run-on sentences by breaking up sentences"

Following discussion of each of the five codes, the chapter concludes by bringing students' perspectives into conversation with Chapter 1's pedagogically focused literature review of flow in writing.

Students' Perspectives: *Idea*

The relatively high frequency of students' quotations coded as *Idea* suggests that students did relate the flow of their writing to their text's meaning. Students commented on meaning in individual sentences, across sentences, and in a text in its entirety. Across quotations, two common themes emerged: making sense and maintaining focus. Students' quotations coded as *Idea* did also occasionally reference repetition, excess information, or too little information as problems that disrupt flow.

For students, the notion of making sense often appeared as part of comments about reading aloud or reviewing some part of the text in an organic, holistic, and/or sensory way. Representative quotations included "I can see if my sentences make sense," "if when I read it out loud it seems to make sense," "I read it out loud and try to make it coherent," "Reread sentences to try and work through it, making sure that it makes sense," and "I reread paragraphs, one at a time, to see if they make sense." Additionally, a few quotations referenced the relationship between a writer and textual meaning. In one such example, the quotation referenced the writer's knowledge: "My knowledge of the topic whether I know it or not." In these cases, the importance of textual meaning to flow was linked to the writer's understanding of their own work. Put differently, whether or not the text flowed depended on whether or not it made sense to the writer.

Making sense did also surface for students as a reader concern, although infrequently. While students regularly commented on giving their writing to someone else to read, only occasionally did they explicitly relate the reader's understanding of the text to flow. In these few cases, students referred to testing out flow by sharing the text with readers, as with "Read it to my friends to see if it makes sense." This also involved the writer imagining the audience's perspective as a means to test making sense and thus flow: "Once reading my essay over I determine if I believe if the reader can understand my point." In general, however, students' comments focused primarily on the writer's understanding of their own meaning, with concern for the reader's understanding surfacing only rarely.

Students' focus on making sense aligns with rhetoricians' descriptions of the overall meaning of a text. Making sense parallels Aristotle's concept of a "whole" in which the parts create one "organic" entity (ca. 350 B.C.E./1994, Part VIII) and, more generally, rhetoricians' emphasis on cohesion, unity, and emphasis (Chaplin, 1984). It also parallels Markels's (1984) focus on coherence and Elbow's emphasis on the natural development of ideas (Elbow, 1998a). Students' responses suggest that the meaning or message they are creating is at the center of their review and revision process, recalling compositionists' emphasis on the organic, holistic development of a unified meaning through engaging with the writing process (Bizzell, 1992; Elbow, 1998a, 1998b; Elbow & Belanoff, 1989; Emig, 1983; Knoblauch & Brannon, 1984; Murray, 1985; Schultz, 1977).

A key difference, however, between students' and scholars' perspectives is the degree to which the reader figures explicitly in discussions of flow. Students rarely referenced the reader's understanding, whereas scholars explicitly discussed and investigated the relationship between the reader's sense of the text's meaning and textual flow (e.g., Booth & Gregory, 1987; Chafe, 1994; Flower, 1993). Put simply, students focused primarily on the writer's role in making meaning, not on the reader's role in working out meaning. Their comments did not embody the idea that writing is an act of communication, a collaborative meaning-making endeavor involving the writer and reader together.

Idea also captured students' quotations about maintaining focus. In some cases, quotations explicitly stated the need to maintain focus, as with the comments, "staying on task with the topic at hand" and "have each paragraph talk about one topic." In other cases, *Idea* captured quotations that referred to the kind or amount of information in a piece of writing, which could work toward or against maintaining focus. Students' comments described the need to reduce or avoid repetition and excess information, such as "don't repeat the point I am trying to get across," "avoiding redundance," "Take out unnecessary filler sentences," and "take things out." Conversely, a few quotations referenced the need to expand information to improve flow: "embed and elaborate on quotes," "analyzing an idea more," "add more details," "Discuss a topic," and "Support ideas with information and examples." These comments on cutting and adding information suggest that students saw the meaning in their writing as a revisable construct that affects flow. This perspective was, however, not common. Most often, students' quotations referenced the ideas already present in the text and how these might be better connected.

Students' quotations coded as *Idea* revealed an interdependence between maintaining focus and connectedness, or how ideas related to an overall theme or to one another, as these quotations illustrate: "If it connects back to [illegible] ideas well and stays on topic," "make sure everything relates to everything else," "I reread my paper to see if all the ideas mesh nicely with each other," "I try to make all of my ideas work together," "Change ideas if needed in order to make them more fitting together," "I make sure ideas are in a logical order," and "ideas are in a logical order." For the students, it seems that maintaining focus depended on how textual meanings related to one another and to the whole text—which suggests an interrelatedness between *Idea* and *Organization*.

The importance of managing connections across ideas became evident when students discussed how they identified or solved problems with flow. In some cases, students described how they identified flow problems, as these quotations suggest: "I read it over out loud or read it to a friend to see if any aspects seem random or introduced,"[1] and "I usually reread the paper to make sure I don't jump from one topic to another abruptly." Not infrequently, comments about staying on topic or not straying included advice, such as "I have been taught to make sure everything fits with your thesis," "topic sentences should fit with rest of the paragraph," "taught to make sure it follow [*sic*] thesis," and "set up first sentence in paragraph as a claim and go from there." As these examples show, this advice was often abstract or formulaic.

Students' concern with maintaining focus or connectedness across ideas aligns in a very basic way with scholars' concern with how information is ordered. Both students and scholars agree that connectedness across ideas enhances flow and that gaining a different perspective on the text (e.g., Flower, 1993), in some cases by reading it aloud (e.g., Elbow & Belanoff, 1995) helps the writer evaluate how effectively ideas are connected. Additionally, students' comments suggest a formulaic approach to connecting information, echoing the early rhetorical tradition that focused on decontextualized models of texts that corresponded to a "mechanistic, skill-based model of composition" (Knoblauch & Brannon, 1984, p. 80).

Interestingly, the advice in formulaic or template-driven students' quotations faintly echoes cognitive schemas or patterns that align with a set of readers' expectations (e.g., Flower, 1993; Hartwell, 1979; Johns, 1997; Podis & Podis, 1990). On some level, when students linked flow to "set[ting] up [*sic*] first sentence in paragraph as a claim" or "topic sentences," they referenced real or idealized patterns that enact "*Recurrent Rhetorical Situations*" (Miller, 1984, p. 155). However, the echo is faint. Absent in students' comments were the crucial links between the typified patterns and the communication situations that motivate the patterns. Overall, students' quotations on maintaining focus and connectedness echo early rhetorical pedagogical approaches.

Students' quotations related to connectedness across ideas do not align with the work of cognitively based compositionists (e.g., Flower, 1979, 1993;

Flower & Hayes, 1980), genre study scholars (e.g., Bazerman, 1995; Miller, 1984; Swales, 1990, 2004), or functional linguists (e.g., Halliday & Martin, 1993; Halliday & Matthiessen, 2013)—all of whom hold up the ways in which a text's purpose and discourse context motivate choices about how to order or relate information. In sum, students and scholars alike recognize that flow depends on creating a sense of wholeness, which, in turn, depends on "the structural union of the parts" (Aristotle, ca. 350 B.C.E./1994, Part VIII). However, while students' quotations do recognize the importance of making sense and maintaining focus or connectedness across ideas, they do not reveal a deep understanding of the relationship between these goals and making purposeful, rhetorically driven choices about how to meet these goals.

Students' Perspectives: *Organization*

Students' quotations indicated that "the organization, order, mapping, sequencing, etc." of information were critical elements of flow (codebook 25). As discussed earlier, *Organization* and *Idea* emerged during coding as intertwined concepts. In keeping with the team's final definitions of *Organization* and *Idea*, a quotation was coded as *Organization* if it discussed some aspect of arrangement; it might or might not have referred to the text's information or ideas. If, however, the information or ideas motivated the mention of arrangement, the quotation was coded as *Idea*.

When students commented on organization alone as a means to create flow, they most often referenced arrangement. On a few occasions, their evaluation of arrangement was based on the senses, such as how a text sounded or felt. Students commented on organization across all levels of an essay: within a sentence, across sentences, and across paragraphs. Overall, two motifs emerged: Students discussed organization without reference to information or ideas, or they did reference information or ideas. When students discussed organization without reference to ideas or information, their comments were generic and, at times, formulaic. When they discussed organization with reference to ideas, their comments were more substantive and more specific.

Students' quotations that focused on internal sentence organization tended to be generic and rarely referenced information or ideas: "I then I [sic] check my sentence structure," "I try to rewrite sentences, to try to restructure them," "I try to reword a sentence," "Try to reword or reorganize the sentence," "change the order of words," and "I look at sentence length along with word choice to make sure my sentences aren't all the same length [sic] choppy [sic] of [sic] run-on . . .." In some cases, the sound of the sentence motivated revision, as with "Change sentences so that they sound better and go with the sentences around them" and "I change the sentence structure to make it sound better."

Interestingly, within single quotations, students rarely mentioned both sentence revision and ideas. One quotation did include rearrangement and ideas, although it did not explicitly relate one to the other: "I try to reconstruct sentences and ideas to make then [sic] flow." In one other quotation, a student explicitly related sentence rearrangement to meaning: "Reread and rearrange my ideas/sentences." These quotations referenced either the sentence as a whole or "words." Notably, they did not discuss phrases and clauses—the information-rich elements of a sentence that are key resources for making meaning through rearrangement. Nor did the quotations specify strategies that might guide decisions about how to order sentence components (e.g., given-new and end-focus expectations).

Students' quotations that focused on organization across sentences without reference to ideas or information were generic or formulaic, as these examples illustrate: "I will try to see if I can move sentences," "switch sentences around," "rearrange words/sentences or delete them," "move a sentence to a different location in the paragraph," and "Sentences at the beginning and end of paragraphs to connect ideas." Similarly, when students commented on organization at the paragraph level without reference to ideas, the substance of their comments was again quite thin: "I may rearrange the order of my paragraphs" and "switching paragraph order."

Although quotations about organization at the sentence and paragraph levels were generic or formulaic, they did suggest that students rearranged text to improve flow and considered sentence and paragraph organization to be important to flow. On the other hand, the revision strategies students described seemed underspecified and disconnected from the reader and the wider rhetorical context. Put differently, they seemed a-rhetorical.

Several quotations coded as *Organization* focused on the writing process. Once again, when no reference was made to ideas or information, the quotations seemed generic, as with the frequent comment "outline." A few quotations referenced ways to begin the writing process, including "plan out the paper before writing it" and "organize using a flow chart/outline." Again, without reference to ideas or information, these strategies seemed to lack the rhetorical awareness that might drive organizational choices.

In sharp contrast to those *Organization* quotations that did not reference ideas, when they did reference ideas, the typical comment was more specific about organizational strategies. Of course, there were still some formulaic comments, such as "Make sure I'm answering questions in [sic] sequence they are given" and "group similar ideas together." More often, however, quotations referenced some aspect of the writing process. In several quotations, organization was referenced as a way to begin the writing process: "It also helps to organize my thoughts before typin g [sic]." In some cases, organization was characterized as a highly structured process, as with "Create a chart, or have your ideas grouped and organized while writing," "I will set up a larger piece of paper and organize my thoughts into the topic of my box," "organize using a flow chart/outline," and "making an outline to place similar ideas together." In other cases, the process was analytical but less structured, as with "Separate out main ideas and see how they are related and what order they should be presented in." In one quotation, the process was particularly intuitive and organic: "Write for a long period of tie [*sic*] and then organize any thoughts." Overall, when quotations coded as *Organization* did reference ideas, they tended to move beyond the generic to hold up specific strategies, some highly structured, some less so.

Students' quotations not only revealed an interdependence between the codes *Organization* and *Idea* but also (to a lesser degree) between *Organization* and *Sensory*, or "how the writer is experiencing their work through senses" (codebook 25). In these cases, the student writer's sense of how a text sounds motivated decisions about arrangement, as these examples illustrate: "I try to rearrange it so that it sounds better together" and "I reword it to make it sound more flowing." Interestingly, how a text "feels" also appeared in one quotation: "see if it all feels right together."[2]

Students' *Organization* quotations align with scholars' concern with organization as an important element of flow. Students and scholars alike address organization at all levels of a text. Students commented on arrangement within and across sentences, as do scholars in functional linguistics and its writing studies counterpart, rhetorical grammar (Gopen & Swan, 1990; Halliday & Matthiessen, 2013; Hancock, 2005; Kolln & Gray, 2017; Noguchi, 1991, 2002; Paraskevas, 2021; Rossen-Knill, 2011, 2013; Salvatore, 2021; Vande Kopple, 1989). In addition, students' quotations occasionally referenced the senses, evoking Elbow's emphasis on the role of the senses in guiding sentence formulations and reformulations (Elbow, 2012). However, while students' quotations do reference both ideas and senses, they do not, on the whole, reflect a rhetorical awareness. They do not, for example, reference the reader's expectations that ground much work in rhetorical grammar. Nor do they evoke Elbow's performative mode or the immersion in the sensory, communicative experience of performing one's work for another.

Students and scholars agree that organization across the essay affects (and effects) flow. Students' comments often focused on structural strategies (e.g., "outline") and on the process of developing and organizing an essay. Overall, comments align with two quite different approaches in the literature: the early rhetoricians' emphasis on established modes of organization, which is perhaps best represented in composition pedagogy by Podis and Podis (1990) and compositionists' emphasis on the organic, intuitive development of the essay, best represented by Elbow (2006) in *The Music of Form*. Once again, however, students' comments do not reflect awareness of the full rhetorical situation, perhaps best represented by writing scholars in genre studies (e.g., Hyland, 2008; Swales, 1990, 2004). Rather, students' organizational choices seem informed by two quite different approaches: on the one hand, static, decontextualized models; on the other hand, the organic development of the writer's meaning and the essay through the writing process.

Students' Perspectives: *Sensory*

In addition to describing flow analytically, students associated it with the senses. This typically involved hearing but also included a more holistic sensory experience. Hearing-oriented quotations coded as *Sensory* often involved reading aloud, such as "I read whatever I'm writing out loud so I can hear the rhythm of my work," "Reading out loud and seeing how the sentences sound," "I read it over out loud to see if it sounds right," and "I read it out loud to myself exactly as I wrote it to correct what doesn't sound correct." However, students sometimes commented on the sound of their work without referencing reading aloud, as in "I try to rearrange it so that it sounds better together" and "I reword it to make it sound more flowing." The notion of how a text "feels" also appeared in a couple of quotations, as in "see if it all feels right together." Whether referencing sound or feeling, these quotations described the sensory experience of flow in a generic manner. Sensory terms referred to a sense as a whole (e.g., feel or sound), as opposed to a more particularized sensory vocabulary.

By contrast, some quotations used specific sensory descriptors to characterize the text, as the following quotes illustrate: "I read it over out loud to myself to see if it sounds choppy or not," "I read my paper out loud to see if it sounds choppy or awkward," "by reading it aloud it doesnt [*sic*] seem choppy, I know I'm effectively flowing," and "Look for choppy and unrelated sentences." By and large, when students used specific language to describe flow, they used negative descriptors that characterized a lack of flow. In one case, a student referenced "elegant wording" as a way to improve flow. However, quotations typically involved little sensory language related to effective flow; when it did appear, it included generic and correctness terms, such as "good," "right," and "correct."

Both students and scholars suggest that sensory elements are a means to experience and troubleshoot the flow of a text. Students relied on the sound of their texts and characterized their work with sensory descriptions of flow (e.g., "choppy"), which aligns with the emphasis on the senses in the works of voice-oriented compositionists (e.g., Booth et al., 2016; Elbow, 1998a, 1998b, 2012; Elbow & Belanoff, 1989, 1995; Rawlins & Metzger, 2009). In general, students do not demonstrate a rich sensory vocabulary and lean toward generic or negative descriptors. Moreover, students' quotations do not convey the *"feels right in the mouth"* quality of a text, that is, that deep, multisensory experience evoked in Elbow's *Vernacular Eloquence* (Elbow, 2012, p. 222).

Students' Perspectives: *Audience Awareness*

Few students' quotations were coded as *Audience Awareness*. Most often, when a quotation referenced the audience's perspective, a generic audience was invoked, either explicitly or implicitly. Examples in which quotations explicitly referenced a generic audience include "consult with other people in case I missed something," "having others read my writing helps," "I have someone else read and revise my papers to get their opinion," and "ask/have someone else read the sentence for suggestions." In the following examples, an audience was referenced only implicitly: "Ask what part seems messy/hard to understand/jumpy" and "Ask someone what I could add to make it sound better." While "ask" in these examples might indicate that there must be someone else at the other end of this communication, the lack of any audience identification again suggests that audience is envisioned as a distant, generic entity.

On occasion, quotations did identify a particular audience, as in the following cases that referenced friends or peers: "Read it to my friends to see if it makes sense," "have a peer or a friend read it and let me know if it feels choppy," "I also try to get help from my peers to see what would sound better," and "have peer reviews so that it is fresh eyes working on your essay." In two quotations, academic writing centers are named as the audience: "I take my paper to the writing center to get antoerh [sic] view and ideas on how to improve" and "ask/have someone else read the sentence for suggestions and go to the writing center." In two cases, a student invoked an imagined audience: "Once reading my essay over I determine if I believe if the reader can understand my point" and "THis [sic] way I can hear first hand how it would sound as if it was being presented." These examples suggest that the writer took on the reader's identity to gain a different perspective on the writing. As the aforementioned quotations illustrate, students' reasons for turning to an audience included wanting to know if the writing "makes sense," if the "idea is getting across," if the text "sounds good" or is "jumpy," and if there was some unspecified feedback that might be followed to improve the flow of the text.

In the relatively few quotations that did discuss themes related to *Audience Awareness*, audience was represented generically; there was no reference to a disciplinary discourse community, a particular nonscholarly group, or a particular reader. Similarly, the feedback writers sought out was underspecified and vague (e.g., "what would sound better" and "read the sentence for suggestions"). Together, the limited mention of audience and the generic quality of references to audience suggest that when considering flow in academic writing, students do not typically recognize the possibility and importance of varied readers. Alternatively, the limited attention to audience may indicate that the writer's meaning takes priority and that flow is an organic process that emerges naturally from a writer's meaning-making process (e.g., Aristotle, ca. 350 B.C.E./1994, Part VIII; Elbow, 1998a). From yet another perspective, it may reflect students' lack of awareness of the relationship between the reader's sense of the text's meaning and textual flow (e.g., Booth & Gregory, 1987; Chafe, 1994; Flower, 1993). There is another possible explanation based in students experience with writing instruction: Perhaps the lack of quotations related to audience reflects, this one years of template-based training. There is, however, still another explanation related to the writing process: Perhaps the time-constrained instructional drafting cycle does not allow the writer enough time to carefully consider readers. In line with Elbow's (1987) suggested process, perhaps writers rightly push their readers out of their minds to focus on developing their own meaning and then, constrained by the course construct, lack the time to sufficiently shift focus toward readers.

Students' Perspectives: *Small Text Unit*

Students' quotations were most often coded as *Small Text Unit*. Put differently, when students commented about creating flow, they most often mentioned textual units "at or below the sentence level (e.g., sentence, clause, phrase, words)"—and, most frequently, they referenced words (codebook 25). Additionally, they often referenced transitions and, less frequently, "punctuation" (codebook 25). Students' references to words typically involved changing words, such as "add or take out words," "reword," "use different vocabulary," and "vary my choices of words." Frequently, the change involved finding a "better" word, with "better" ranging from abstract advice such as "use better word choice" to the slightly more specific "add more exciting words" or "I try to include more elegant wording." In one case, the student seemed to relate word changes to creating "correct" sentences, that is, sentences that conform to an accepted standard: "I would substitute words/phrases to make the sentence sound more like a real sentence." In contrast to this correctness view, another student related changing words to better representing their own meaning: "Use better word choice and try to fix the sentence to exactly what I want to say."

Students' emphasis on word-level changes overlaps with writing handbooks' emphasis on words. In one representative handbook, *The Brief Penguin Handbook* (Faigley, 2003), the part on "Effective Style and Language" indexed several sections that center on words, including "use action verbs," "name your agents," "eliminate unnecessary words," and "reduce wordy phrases," as well as a section on tone and register titled "Find the right words" ("Contents"). Students' *Small Text Unit* quotations also align with specific handbook advice about concision, precision, simplicity, word choice, and creating the right tone. For example, handbook advice to "ELIMINATE UNNECESSARY WORDS" (Faigley, 2003, p. 332) resonates in the students' comment "take out words." Additionally, handbook advice on being precise can be heard in student comments such as "Use better word choice and try to fix the sentence to exactly what I want to say," "more elegant wording," and "add more exciting words."

Although handbooks such as those discussed in the literature review do give decontextualized advice related to sentence structure patterns, students' comments do not reflect this advice. Students' quotations do not, for example, echo *The Everyday Writer*'s (Lunsford, 2013) sections on "Coordination,

Subordination, and Emphasis"; "Parallelism"; "Shifts" related to tense, mood, or voice; and "Sentence Variety" (p. 268). The emphasis in students' quotations on discrete words—rather than on meaning-rich phrase- and clause-level patterns—recalls Sommers's (1980) well-known description of the less-experienced writer who, in comparison to the experienced writer, does not make meaningful sentence-level revisions, but rather limits revision to changing words and making other micro-edits.

"Words" also surfaced in students' quotations that point to transitions as a way to create flow. However, quotations about transitions also referenced larger structures. Transitions were linked to the sentence as a whole ("transition sentences"), as well as to paragraphs ("transitions of paragraphs"). In addition, quotations related transitions to meaning. For example, students referenced them as a way to manage ideas ("Constantly include transitions to keep deas [sic] connected" or "I look to use transitional words or sentences to introduce new ideas"). Students' quotations also discussed transitions as part of past-learned advice, such as "I have been taught to include transitions" or "I've been taught to use transitions." In some quotations, the advice seemed to echo a learned formula, so much so that we marked these as "formulaic." Typical examples include decontextualized template-like strategies that call for "Sentences at the beginning and end of paragraphs to connect ideas" and "Transitions at the beginning in sentences."

Students' concern with sentence-level transitions aligns well with some writing instruction texts and websites. As do students' quotations, writing texts and websites (as discussed in chapter 1) vary not only in the degree to which they discuss flow explicitly but also in the extent to which the discussion addresses rhetorical influences. The students' focus on transitions also relates to scholarly and pedagogical work in metadiscourse—as noted earlier, "those aspects of the text that embody writer-reader interactions" (Hyland & Tse, 2004, p. 159). Transitions are one of several kinds of metadiscourse that guide readers through texts and help them relate one idea to another (e.g., Graff & Birkenstein, 2021; Hyland & Tse, 2004), thus supporting a smooth reading experience.

One might also have expected students to mention other types of metadiscourse that connect ideas and guide the reader through the text, such as "frame markers," which "refer to discourse acts, sequences, or text stages" (e.g., "finally/to conclude/my purpose here is to") or markers that refer to parts within the text (e.g., "noted above") or to outside references (e.g., "according to") (Hyland & Tse, 2004, p. 169). However, in students' comments, "transitions" was the dominant term for textual linkages. Students' lack of discussion of other kinds of metadiscourse suggests that they do not have explicit knowledge of the range of metadiscourse markers. Students' quotations further suggest that they do not have explicit knowledge of metadiscourse as a tool to create flow in writing. This is not surprising since metadiscourse is just making its way into mainstream/popular writing texts, most notably *They*

Say/I Say (Graff & Birkenstein, 2021), and even the somewhat rhetorically minded University of North Carolina at Chapel Hill website, which continues to use *transitions* as an overarching term for kinds of connectors (The Writing Center at the University of North Carolina at Chapel Hill, 2023).

When students commented on sentence punctuation as a means to improve flow, they typically referenced it vaguely or with respect to correctness. Representative responses to prompts about how to improve flow ranged from the minimal response "punctuation" to vague comments such as "change punctuations [*sic*]," "use different punctuations [*sic*]," and "fix punctuation." In several cases, the responses involved generic, prescriptive advice, such as "use less commans [*sic*]," "use the punctuations [*sic*] correctly," and "edit any comma splices or misuse of colons."

Students' comments align with student handbook discussions of how to use punctuation correctly. Generally absent are comments about punctuation's rhetorical purposes that appeared, for example, in The St. Martin's Handbook Instructor's Notes (Lunsford, 2011)—but not in the student companion text (Lunsford, 2011). In line with student handbook overviews of punctuation, students' quotations do not typically discuss a punctuation mark's particular function or mention punctuation as a means to manage ideas, create rhetorical effects, or shape the text's prosody or sensory experience. In this way, students' quotations about punctuation differ significantly from work that explicitly relates punctuation to the reading experience and meaning of text (e.g., Chafe, 1994; Hancock, 2005; Kolln & Gray, 2017).

Overall, students' *Small Text Unit* quotations align well with process-based pedagogy (e.g., Flower, 1979; Flower & Hayes, 1981) and handbook-type advice that recommends addressing sentence-level editing at the end of the writing process in order to write proper sentences. In line with the process approach, students' comments suggest that they did not view sentence-level revision as a particularly meaningful part of the writing process, but rather as a proofing step aimed at small, correctness-focused changes that, while relevant to flow, have little impact on meaning.

Students' quotations do not align with writing texts that grow out of functional linguistics (Aull, 2015b; Hancock, 2005; Kolln & Gray, 2017; Lancaster, 2012; Vande Kopple, 1989), all of which emphasize rhetorical motivations for making sentence-level choices. Nor do they even align with the limited advice from one well-known writing center website that has begun to incorporate insights from functional grammar and the related rhetorical grammar (e.g., University of North Carolina at Chapel Hill, 2023). As Hancock (2005) explains, "It [formal grammar] pretends that the decisions we are making about revising our sentences have nothing to do with the situation of the writing or the sentences that precede and follow the sentence in question" (p. 176).

In general, this decontextualized approach seems to permeate students' *Small Text Unit* quotations, which are frequently vague and an apparent echo of decontextualized advice about writing correct sentences. Students' emphasis on a-rhetorical, correctness-based changes may result from a history of writing instruction that privileges decontextualized correctness. This prioritization overlooks the writer's role in making rhetorically based sentence-level changes that affect textual flow and the readers' perception of flow. Students may also lack explicit language to talk about the sentence, which, in turn, might prevent them from discussing the relationship between sentence-level choices and meaning or the sentence-level elements that contribute to flow.

Convergences and Divergences

Considered together, students' quotations, much like the scholars' perspectives presented in Chapter 1, point to similar textual and rhetorical elements to account for flow in writing: the writer's meaning, ideas, and organization as distinct but highly intertwined/interdependent; the sensory experience—or qualia—of writing; sentence-level elements; and the reader. However, the students' perspectives align most closely with two seemingly contradictory pedagogies that grow out of traditional (early) rhetoric: the writer-focused, organic process pedagogy and decontextualized arrangements or rules that support a cohesive and coherent text.

Students' *Idea* quotations most obviously parallel process pedagogy concerns with enabling the writer's innate/implicit ability to discover, develop, and communicate their meanings. This approach can also be felt in *Sensory* quotations and the generic (nonanalytical) nature of students' quotations about, for example, arrangement. In contrast to this organic, natural process, students' comments also bring to mind decontextualized advice in relation to structure (e.g., use topic sentences), information management (e.g., avoid repetition), and style (e.g., avoid passive voice). Importantly, students' quotations do suggest that organization is linked to meaning, but this typically involves the writer's meaning rather than an awareness of or concern with how the reader is making meaning. Similarly, students' quotations do recognize the presence of audience, but typically as a generic presence or a source of general feedback.

In stark contrast to the chorus of writer-focused pedagogies heard in students' quotations, reader-based pedagogies do not leave even a faint echo. Students' comments do not suggest explicit awareness of a particularized audience or of readers who bring a history of language use and experiences; nor do they suggest awareness of the rhetorical situation, either as it relates to the discourse context or textual choices. With respect to sentence-level choices, students' quotations do not discuss rhetorical strategies that shape the writer's meaning and draw on readers' expectations or interpretations in order to improve flow. In fact, students' quotations suggest that they are not familiar with a substantial part of the pedagogy literature related to flow, specifically genre work, as well as work in functional and rhetorical grammar.

There are several possible reasons for the apparent absence of reader-based pedagogies: The students' instructors were familiar with writer-focused pedagogies but less so with reader-based pedagogies; the students were raised on process pedagogy and decontextualized advice and continued to draw on what they'd previously learned; course or program curricula relevant to this study favored writer-focused pedagogies to the detriment of reader-focused pedagogies; students did not have time for their writing process to naturally become more reader-focused; students did not recognize their classroom writing as a rhetorical act; and/or the writing assignment did not include a sufficiently real audience. No doubt there are other reasons, but the absence of reader-based strategies remains striking. For this reason, we return to it in our final section on the pedagogical implications of our work.

Notes

1. Underlines indicate the part of a quotation that maps onto the code.
2. Although "see" is used in this last and other student quotations, it's meaning was not clearly related to engagement with the visual senses. That said, "see" did occur several times in conjunction with another sense, such as "see if it sounds," as well as in such constructions as "see if it makes sense." Because the coding team could not distinguish this use from a meaning like "find out," we determined not to code these instances as *Sensory*. That said, there remains something intriguing about a sensory verb being conventionalized as a way to experience the text.

References

Aristotle. (1994). *Poetics* (S. H. Butcher, Trans.). The Internet Classics Archive. http://classics.mit.edu/Aristotle/poetics.1.1.html (Original work published ca. 350 B.C.E.)

Aull, L. (2015b). Linguistic attention in rhetorical genre studies and first year writing. *Composition Forum, 31*. https://compositionforum.com/issue/31/linguistic-attention.php

Bazerman, C. (1995). *The informed writer: Using sources in the disciplines* (5th ed.). Houghton Mifflin.

Bizzell, P. (1992). What is a discourse community? In *Academic discourse and critical consciousness* (pp. 222–237). University of Pittsburgh Press. https://doi.org/10.2307/j.ctt7zwb7k.14

Booth, W. C., Colomb, G. G., Williams, J. M., Bizup, J., & FitzGerald, W. T. (2016). *The craft of research* (4th ed.). University of Chicago Press.

Booth, W. C., & Gregory, M. W. (1987). *The Harper and Row rhetoric: Writing as thinking, thinking as writing*. Harper & Row.

Chafe, W. (1994). *Discourse, consciousness, and time: The flow and displacement of conscious experience in speaking and writing*. University of Chicago Press.

Chaplin, M. T. (1984). Foreword. In R. B. Markels (Ed.), *A new perspective on cohesion in expository paragraphs* (pp. vii–ix). Southern Illinois University Press.

Corbin, J. M., & Strauss, A. (1990). Grounded theory research: Procedures, canons, and evaluative criteria. *Qualitative Sociology, 13*(1), 3–21. https://doi.org/10.1007/BF00988593

Elbow, P. (1987). Closing my eyes as I speak: An argument for ignoring audience. *College English, 49*(1), 50–69. https://doi.org/10.2307/377789

Elbow, P. (1998a). *Writing with power: Techniques for mastering the writing process* (2nd ed.). Oxford University Press.

Elbow, P. (1998b). *Writing without teachers* (2nd ed.). Oxford University Press.

Elbow, P. (2006). The music of form: Rethinking organization in writing. *College Composition and Communication, 57*(4), 620–666.

Elbow, P. (2012). *Vernacular eloquence: What speech can bring to writing*. Oxford University Press.

Elbow, P., & Belanoff, P. (1989). *A community of writers: A workshop course in writing* (1st ed.). Random House.

Elbow, P., & Belanoff, P. (1995). *Sharing and responding* (3rd ed.). McGraw-Hill Higher Education.

Emig, J. (1983). *The web of meaning: Essays on writing, teaching, learning, and thinking* (D. Goswami & M. Butler, Eds.). Boynton/Cook Publishers.

Faigley, L. (2003). *The brief penguin handbook*. Pearson Education.

Flower, L. (1979). Writer-based prose: A cognitive basis for problems in writing. *College English, 41*(1), 19–37. https://doi.org/10.2307/376357

Flower, L. (1993). *Problem-solving strategies for writing* (4th ed.). Harcourt Brace Jovanovich College Publishers.

Flower, L., & Hayes, J. R. (1980). The cognition of discovery: Defining a rhetorical problem. *College Composition and Communication, 31*(1), 21–32. https://doi.org/10.2307/356630

Flower, L., & Hayes, J. R. (1981). A cognitive process theory of writing. *College Composition and Communication, 32*(4), 365–387. http://dx.doi.org/10.2307/356600

Gopen, G. D., & Swan, J. A. (1990). The science of scientific writing. *American Scientist, 78*(6), 550–558.

Graff, G., & Birkenstein, C. (2010). *They say/I say: The moves that matter in academic writing* (2nd ed.). W. W. Norton & Company.

Graff, G., & Birkenstein, C. (2021). *They say/I say: The moves that matter in academic writing* (5th ed.). W. W. Norton & Company.

Halliday, M. A. K., & Martin, J. R. (1993). *Writing science: Literacy and discursive power*. Routledge. https://doi-org/10.4324/9780203209936

Halliday, M. A. K., & Matthiessen, C. M. (2013). *Halliday's introduction to functional grammar* (4th ed.). Routledge. https://doi-org/10.4324/9780203431269

Hancock, C. (2005). *Meaning-centered grammar: An introductory text*. Equinox.

Hartwell, P. (1979). Teaching arrangement: A pedagogy. *College English, 40*(5), 548–554. https://doi.org/10.2307/376327

Hyland, K. (2008). Genre and academic writing in the disciplines. *Language Teaching, 41*(4), 543–562. https://doi.org/10.1017/S0261444808005235

Hyland, K., & Tse, P. (2004). Metadiscourse in academic writing: A reappraisal. *Applied Linguistics, 25*(2), 156–177. https://doi.org/10.1093/applin/25.2.156

Johns, A. M. (1997). *Text, role, and context: Developing academic literacies.* Cambridge University Press.

Knoblauch, C. H., & Brannon, L. (1984). *Rhetorical traditions and the teaching of writing.* Boynton/Cook Publishers.

Kolln, M., & Gray, L. (2017). *Rhetorical grammar: Grammatical choices, rhetorical effects.* Pearson.

Lancaster, C. I. (2012). *Stance and reader positioning in upper-level student writing in political theory and economics.* [Doctoral dissertation, University of Michigan]. Deep Blue Documents. https://deepblue.lib.umich.edu/handle/2027.42/93976

Lunsford, A. A. (2011). *The St. Martin's handbook* (7th ed.). Bedford/St. Martin's.

Lunsford, A. A. (2013). *The everyday writer: Instructor's edition* (5th ed.). Bedford/St. Martin's.

Markels, R. B. (1984). *A new perspective on cohesion in expository paragraphs.* Southern Illinois University Press.

Miller, C. R. (1984). Genre as social action. *Quarterly Journal of Speech, 70*(2), 151–167. https://doi.org/10.1080/00335638409383686

Murray, D. M. (1985). *A writer teaches writing* (2nd ed.). Houghton Mifflin.

Noguchi, R. R. (1991). *Grammar and the teaching of writing: Limit and possibilities.* NCTE.

Noguchi, R. R. (2002). Rethinking the teaching of grammar. *The English Record, 52*(2), 22–26.

Paraskevas, C. C. (2021). *Exploring grammar through texts: Reading and writing the structure of English.* Routledge.

Podis, J. M., & Podis, L. A. (1990). Identifying and teaching rhetorical plans for arrangement. *College Composition and Communication, 41*(4), 430–442. https://doi.org/10.2307/357932

Rawlins, J., & Metzger, S. (2009). *The writer's way* (7th ed.). Houghton Mifflin.

Rossen-Knill, D. F. (2011). Flow and the principle of relevance: Bringing our dynamic speaking knowledge to writing. *Journal of Teaching Writing, 26*(1), 39–67. https://journals.iupui.edu/index.php/teachingwriting/article/view/26270/24281

Rossen-Knill, D. F. (2013). Refining the given-new expectation for classroom use: A lesson in the importance of audience. *Journal of Teaching Writing, 28*(1), 21–51. https://journals.iupui.edu/index.php/teachingwriting/article/view/20717/20250

Rossen-Knill, D. F., & Bakhmetyeva, T. (2011). *Including students in academic conversations: Principles and strategies for teaching theme-based writing courses across the disciplines.* Hampton Press.

Saldaña, J. (2009). *The coding manual for qualitative researchers.* SAGE Publications.

Salvatore, J. (2021). Tools, not rules: Rhetorical grammar as a meaning-making tool in the creative writing workshop. *Journal of Teaching Writing, 36*(1), 91–128. https://journals.iupui.edu/index.php/teachingwriting/article/view/26242/24359

Schultz, J. (1977). The story workshop method: Writing from start to finish. *College English, 39*(4), 411–436. https://doi.org/10.2307/375765

Sommers, N. (1980). Revision strategies of student writers and experienced adult writers. *College Composition and Communication, 31*(4), 378–388. https://doi.org/10.2307/356588

Swales, J. M. (1990). *Genre analysis: English in academic and research settings* (C. A. Chapelle & S. Hunston, Eds.). Cambridge University Press.

Swales, J. M. (2004). *Research genres: Explorations and applications* (M. H. Long & J. C. Richards, Ed.). Cambridge University Press.

Vande Kopple, W. (1989). *Clear and coherent prose.* Scott, Foresman and Company.

Williams, J. M. (2003). *Style: Ten lessons in clarity and grace* (7th ed.). Addison-Wesley Educational Publishers.

The Writing Center at the University of North Carolina at Chapel Hill. (2023). *Flow.* University of North Carolina at Chapel Hill. https://writingcenter.unc.edu/tips-and-tools/flow/

3 What Do Instructors Say?

We've seen how students think about flow, but what do their instructors say about it? What do they say about how it is conceived, felt, taught, and assessed in student writing? As part of our larger flow study, we sought out feedback from instructors, all of whom taught first-year writing at one of two private liberal arts colleges in the Northeastern United States of loosely equivalent size and rank. We solicited instructors' interest through each institution's intermediary writing program administrator. Eleven instructors across both institutions ultimately opted to participate in the study. Of the total number of instructor-participants, four identified as male, while the rest seven identified as female. With respect to racial demographics, 10 of the 11 instructor-participants identified their race/ethnicity as "Caucasian," with one instructor-participant identifying as "Hispanic and Caucasian." All instructors indicated that English is their primary language, though 1 of the 11 instructors stated they are also fluent in French. With regards to their academic training and current departmental affiliations, one had a JD and primarily worked in a prelaw program. The other 10 cited training and current teaching in English departments, though within this domain, there were a variety of specializations: for example, rhetoric, communication studies, 18th-century British literature. The instructors were randomly selected into one of three flow pedagogy groups: an instruction-as-usual group, in which the instructor taught flow in their course in their customary fashion (even if that meant no instruction altogether), a group that used a voice approach based on the work of Peter Elbow (2012), or a group that used a rhetorical grammar approach inspired by the work of scholars like Halliday and Hasan (1976), Kolln and Gray (2017), and Rossen-Knill (2011, 2013). Of the 11 instructor-participants, two were assigned to the instruction-as-usual group, four were assigned to the voice group, and five were assigned to the rhetorical grammar group.

Once the groups were established, instructors met with a faculty trainer from our research team to go over the study's expectations. For those in the instruction-as-usual group, the trainer simply provided a brief overview of the study's purpose and logistics. For those assigned to either the voice or rhetorical grammar group, the faculty trainer similarly provided an overview of the

66 What Do Instructors Say?

study and its logistics. Alongside this overview, the trainer also provided the two conditioned groups with training on the techniques and instructional materials relevant to their instructional group. Please note that instructor surveys and instructional materials are available on request; slightly revised versions of instructional materials may be found in the Appendix.

Both prior to the study's onset and after its conclusion, researchers asked instructor-participants to broadly reflect on their schematizations of flow through pre- and post-surveys. The pre-survey featured an array of questions about the ways in which the instructors defined and operationalized flow. It inquired about what instruction on flow (if any) instructors had received, how they optimized flow in their own writing, and how they characteristically taught flow (if at all) to their students. The post-survey similarly addressed definitional matters pertaining to flow but focused more on instructional techniques, with special attention given to the instructors' perceptions of the affordances and limitations of the voice and rhetorical grammar approaches. After they completed the post-surveys, instructors in the voice and rhetorical grammar groups were interviewed by the faculty trainer assigned to assist each group. The interview aimed to further distill insights gleaned from the post-survey about the instructors' perspectives on the affordances and limitations of using their assigned instructional method (i.e., voice or rhetorical grammar) and to learn whether their experience teaching with the assigned instructional method altered the ways in which they might frame discussions of flow in future classes.

The majority of the data in this chapter emerged from statements provided in the pre-survey as this was a more capacious space for instructors to reflect widely on flow, the historical patterns of how they were taught flow, and how they broached flow in their own classrooms. As such, unless otherwise explicitly stated, all instructor statements presented in this chapter were drawn from their comments in the pre-survey. It is also important to note that instructors' names were altered to protect anonymity. For each instructor, the study team assigned a pseudonym that naturalistically substituted for their natal names. Lastly, gender pronouns displayed throughout the chapter reflect the gender identities that the instructors self-designated on the demographic portion of the pre-survey.

In general, analysis of the data from our surveys and interviews revealed an overarching instructor narrative that dovetailed with the inconsistencies revealed in the literature review's depiction of flow, namely, "flow" denotes an experience of a text (or a reading experience) that we crave and that factors into instructor grading decisions (Aull, 2015; Knoblauch & Brannon, 1984; North, 2005). Yet, the concept was (and continues to be) highly nebulous—perhaps stemming from its lack of semantic fixity and the multidisciplinarity of writing studies. The slippery nature of flow as a concept, its tendency to trouble a singularity of definition, renders it difficult to operationalize in the classroom (Flower, 1993). Tellingly, this tension between affirming the importance of flow while simultaneously lacking a clear schema or pedagogical approach to it appeared to be fairly ubiquitous, long-standing, and cross-generational.

In the main, our instructors indicated that their uncertainty around flow related to myopias in their own writing pedagogy training, which generally failed to provide them with any tangible methods for conceptualizing or teaching flow. A dearth in training on flow emerged as a clear trope. This recurrence of absence played out in the majority of instructor responses to the pre-survey question, "How were you taught to improve flow in your own academic writing?" One instructor, Andrew, provided this incisive response: "Haphazardly? I honestly don't remember the word 'flow' being used in any course I took." Such feelings echoed throughout the majority of instructors' responses. Linda stated, "I don't think I was taught to improve flow," a conviction shared by Barbara, who likewise said, "I don't recall being taught flow." Insofar as instructors recollected any formal training in their own educational backgrounds on flow, it tended to be rule-based. Steven posited, "I don't recal [sic] much formal instruction, although I do remember being advised to begin a new paragraph by using a phrase or idea fro [sic] the end of the previous one." In effect, Steven's words suggest a general pedagogical inattention paid to matters of flow in writing outside a few (under-explained) exhortations to conform to pre-established writerly rules. In a sense, Andrew's characterization of his instructional training around flow as "haphazard" benchmarks a significant number of the instructors' experiences: On the one hand, they tended to have minimal or no formal education about what flow signified or how to assess flow; on the other hand, they implicitly realized that it signified a great deal with respect to the construction and reception of effective writing.

Although instructors did not recollect[1] training on flow in their own educational backgrounds, they generally made such instruction a part of the pedagogical ecosystem of their own classrooms. This begs the following question: If instructors did not appreciably learn about flow from their own educational backgrounds, what were the sources of their flow-based pedagogical practices? This was not easily discernible from surveys and interviews. That said, the instructors' comments did reveal a number of themes, with two being particularly prominent: 1) There are a cluster of approaches for teaching flow in the classroom; 2) there is a marked disconnect between how instructors teach flow to their students and how they operationalize it in their own work.

The first theme reveals a pedagogical gap: Despite their own perceived lack of explicit training in flow as students, the large majority of instructors said that they did, in fact, teach flow. Instructors' feedback indicated that even though they often struggled to articulate a coherent notion of flow as a concept, they did deploy a varied repertoire of practices in their classrooms to help pinpoint and untangle issues with flow. Some instructors, like Jennifer and Stacey, preferred using an organic, holistic approach such as "reading aloud." Some others used graphic models like outlining, though as Barbara claimed, despite the utility of such graphic approaches to flow, outlines were frequently "resisted by students." The majority preferred the types of sentence-level alterations supported by textbooks. For instance, Anne and Steven used the "'As a Result': *Connecting the Parts*" chapter of *They Say/I Say* (Graff & Birkenstein, 2014) to provide students with concrete models that would enable them to identify and revise textual elements to enhance the experience of flow. Per the advice of Graff and Birkenstein, this took the form of employing four key "strategies": "1) using transition terms. . . . 2) adding pointing words. . . . 3) developing a set of key terms and phrases. . . . 4) repeating yourself but with a difference" (p. 108). As Graff and Birkenstein would have it, if these strategies are actively adopted, students' texts will better effect what Csikszentmihalyi (1990) calls a flow state in readers. Even for those who did not overtly allude to textbook usage, the majority (10 of the 11 instructors) focused on micro-elements, like transitions, to help ameliorate flow problems in student writing. Such approaches were the primary method of instruction for 9 of the 11 instructors. These sentence-level methods were captured in Steven's work on transitions with his students, in which he foregrounded "identifying key repeated words; using transition words/phrases; pointing words." Steven did also indicate that he drew on Graff and Birkenstein's *They Say/I Say*.

To repeat, the upshot seems to be that even though instructors themselves did not have explicit instruction in creating flow, they employed pedagogical techniques for helping students navigate flow concerns. Moreover, our data spoke to two distinct (and often binary) approaches used by instructors to teach flow: a macro-level holistic, organic approach to flow in the vein of compositionists like Peter Elbow (2012) or a more prescriptive, micro-level sentence-based approach. Typically, instructors used one or the other, but two instructors utilized both. At the macro-level (a whole text), instructors suggested that unity and organization were innately conceivable constructs. At the micro-level (paragraphs, sentences, phrases), instructors viewed flow as more mechanical, less meaningful, and hence best solved by a set of prescribed rules. Perhaps in a correlative fashion, there did not seem to be much interweaving of practices that conceptualized flow as a matter of global, idea-based meaning with flow as a series of sentences meant to glue the past, present, and future elements of the text together. Revealingly, prior to the study, only one instructor, Steven (who signaled skepticism about voice-based approaches to flow), had previously used linguistics-based approaches in his writing instruction. He highlighted the utility of George Gopen's (2004) *The Sense of Structure*—namely, its paradigm of "connecting sentences head to head or head to tails." With the exception of Steven, no instructors appeared to practice, or even be cognizant of, rhetorical grammar approaches to flow.

These preferences for holistic, organic approaches and/or prescriptivist sentence-level work may stem from the disciplinary backgrounds of instructors—with the majority identifying as humanists. Such positionings might speak to the relative lack of conceptualizing or teaching flow from the perspectives of more technical discursive domains like linguistics or cognitive science. Instructors' comments suggested that the disciplinary background mattered, and yet, this alone did not fully account for instructional choices. Steven comes from an English literature background, yet he perceived the organic, holistic approach as "romantic" and preferred linguistics-informed methods. This is all to say that narratives around flow and writing pedagogy are complex. They are influenced by many (potentially competing) variables: our training, our disciplines, our personal learning preferences, and the priorities in a field at any particular historical moment.

Notably, the narratives that emerged from instructors' anecdotal perceptions about their instructional experiences with flow as students and as teachers tended to align with the larger findings in our literature review. For instance, the literature review highlighted that historically, popular pedagogical tools have overlooked matters of flow, although some newer resources do offer limited coverage (Glenn & Gray, 2017; Graff & Birkenstein, 2014; Hacker & Sommers, 2021; Lunsford, 2019). Yet, as the literature on flow and instructor-participant feedback both demonstrate, the concept of flow and the consequent practice around it lack coherence. While the literature review indicates that contemporary primers did often include language related to flow, the references were tangential (or "haphazard" to borrow instructor Andrew's parlance), without a full expansion on the multidimensionality of the concept. Instructors' comments indicated that difficulties with teaching flow stem from a lack of conceptual clarity around it, a phenomenon echoed in the literature review. This plurality of definitions seems, as the literature review posited, to relate to the disparate disciplinary perspectives that serve as wellsprings for composition studies. Some prevailing (if unresolved) tensions can be embodied in the following representative questions: Is flow microstructural or macrostructural? Is flow about coherence and cohesion (Booth & Gregory, 1987)? Are these concepts distinguishable or are they collapsible, as Vande Kopple (1989) contends? Does the concept reside in the writer's text (Knoblauch & Brannon, 1984), the reader's encounter with it (Chafe, 1994; Csikszentmihalyi, 1990; Flower, 1993), or both (Johns, 1997)? Do we achieve flow through a classical–rhetoric–inflected Platonic ideal of a unity of textual forms (Knoblauch & Brannon, 1984) or through employing generic or pragmatic approaches to organization (Kuriloff, 1996)? These questions arise from flow's fugitive meaning and seem open to any and all interpretations based on the particular perspective of the user invoking the term.

Whereas the first theme reveals a pedagogical gap, the second theme exposes a disconnect between how instructors taught flow to their students and how they managed it in their own writing. Andrew, for example, foregrounded "subordination" and "linking words" in classroom exercises about flow. However, in his own work, he relied on "outlining at [a] more macro level" and "reading aloud at [a] more micro level." Similarly, Anne's pedagogical and personal approaches diverged. With respect to classroom instruction, Anne indicated a propensity toward "transitions and templates from *They Say/I Say*." Yet, in her own work, she prioritized "revision" and "reading aloud." Linda likewise tended to prioritize "transition" and "strategies to move between ideas and paragraphs" with her students, whereas she specified reading "sentences for connecting logic and style" in her own writerly practice.

As with the first theme, this disconnect between instructors' own writing practices and their instructional practices is recurrent, but not universal. There are important counternarratives. Steven, the only instructor who came into the study using rhetorical grammar approaches, highlighted his use of Gopen's (2004) seminal work on given-new and end-focus, *The Sense of Structure*, both with his students and in his own work. However, as a general principle, instructors' feedback suggested that they did not bring the strategies they used in their own work to their classroom instruction on flow.

Whereas in their own work, instructors largely conceived of flow as a matter of overall meaning, in their classrooms, they typically deployed approaches that focused on correcting sentences. These discontinuities may emanate from perceptions of developmental differences in writing—real and assumed—between instructors as experienced writers and students as beginners. In her influential "Revision Strategies of Student Writers and Experienced Adult Writers," Nancy Sommers (1980) tracked the divergence in revision (both as a concept and practice) between experienced writers and less-experienced student writers. Sommers found that student writers did not manage prospective readers' expectations or globally rework writing, in contrast to experienced writers, who were mindful of readers' expectations and revising to shape global meaning. Sommers's comparison of student and experienced writers may explain some of the divide in how instructors approached flow in their own writing relative to how they did so with students in introductory writing courses. In his post-study survey, Michael articulated the difference between first-year and experienced writers as the basis for his chosen instructional strategies:

> In [his first-year writing courses] I do not go into that level of depth [on flow instruction] because there are more significant global issues to deal with more novice freshmen writers with much more varied abilities than the students enrolled in the [upper-level writing courses].

Perhaps other instructors also sense that a sentence-level, mechanistic approach might be easier for novice writers to digest. Inversely, instructors, being aware that student writers may be grappling with many substantive higher-order issues and pressed to teach writing in already time-strapped courses, might have felt that they lacked the time to provide scaffolding around the nuanced and sophisticated ways flow might arise across the intertwined micro- and macro-layers of writing. Thus, it may be that instructors generally precluded practices that were perceived to be more time-consuming and/or sophisticated but used these practices in their own writing because they were more experienced, had greater facility with the writing process and rhetorical principles, and had more time to write and revise.

To sum up, instructors' reflections on flow conveyed a nuanced (at times, even contradictory) story regarding the way it was articulated and taught in the classroom. Our research suggests that the instructors in our study were trying to actualize Flower's (1993) clarion call for "a more practical, operational definition of 'flow'" (p. 284), but not really succeeding. Success is difficult, however, because the field still lacks a coherent operational definition of flow. Instructors in our study clearly entered the classroom without much training on flow and without many dedicated resources that can be implemented in classroom pedagogy. Additionally, instructors frequently commented on classroom practices on flow that were decentered from their own set of practices. This study's instructor narrative is thus one of marked ambivalence: On the one hand, instructors recognized that flow deeply impacts the quality of student writing and, as a result, necessitated classroom attention. On the other hand, instructors expressed discomfort teaching flow because they did not feel fully comfortable defining it or locating resources to help assimilate flow instruction in the classroom context.

The data posited further tropes. For one, instructors (excepting Steven) did not indicate exposure to linguistics-based training on flow at the level of the essay, paragraph (schema), or sentence-level constructions (rhetorical grammar).[2] Without a linguistics-based approach, instructors may have had limited tools to help students less able to rely on sensory approaches suggested by Elbow (2012) such as those from diverse ability and sociolinguistic backgrounds. Steven, in his post-study interview, highlighted such a scenario when he expressed skepticism that grammar is "intuitive and inherent" for every writer. Another trend that emerged, perhaps as a consequence of the lack of training in linguistic approaches to flow, was a de-linking of global matters of arrangement/coherence from smaller-scale, sentence-level cohesion. The data suggested that instructors either foregrounded flow as a matter of large-scale organization and unity, indebted to rhetoricians like Aristotle (ca. 350 B.C.E./1994), or in their words, they had students "fix" sentences by adding "linking words" or "transitions." In de-linking meaning and the sentence, instructional practices gravitated toward prescriptivism. Absent were strategies that linked sentence-level constructions to global facets of flow; neither was there instruction on how sentence-level constructions afford writers choices that shape their meaning and create more or less effective reading experiences. While meaningful practices were more apparent in instructors' comments about their own writing (even if they did not have formal training in linguistics), it did not typically carry over to classroom pedagogy on flow.

Significantly, such findings redoubled what we noted, both in our literature review and data from students, that flow is simultaneously highly cited and ineffable, both everywhere and nowhere in our writing classrooms. It is the writing concept that dare not speak its definition.

Notes

1. It is possible that instructors did learn about flow at some point in their educational training but have simply forgotten or misremembered these experiences. In their work on transfer and integration in a longitudinal context, Smith et al. (2021), transfer and negative transfer are shaped by our "writing stories," essentially schemas or narratives we hold about our writing. Such writing stories selectively shape what we remember and how we characterize our experiences in relation to our writing.
2. Notably, the instructors in our study are all native English speakers. Non-native English-speaking instructors whose English education involved extensive instruction in English grammar may be more likely to draw from and prefer linguistics-based approaches to flow.

References

Aristotle. (1994). *Poetics* (S. H. Butcher, Trans.). The Internet Classics Archive. http://classics.mit.edu/Aristotle/poetics.1.1.html (Original work published ca. 350 B.C.E.)

Aull, L. (2015). *First-year university writing: A corpus-based study with implications for pedagogy*. Palgrave Macmillan.

Booth, W. C., & Gregory, M. W. (1987). *The Harper and Row rhetoric: Writing as thinking, thinking as writing*. Harper & Row.

Chafe, W. (1994). *Discourse, consciousness, and time: The flow and displacement of conscious experience in speaking and writing*. University of Chicago Press.

Csikszentmihalyi, M. (1990). *Flow: The psychology of optimal experience* (1st ed.). Harper & Row.

Elbow, P. (2012). *Vernacular eloquence: What speech can bring to writing*. Oxford University Press.

Flower, L. (1993). *Problem-solving strategies for writing* (4th ed.). Harcourt Brace Jovanovich College Publishers.

Glenn, C., & Gray, L. (2017). *The Hodges Harbrace handbook* (19th ed.). Cengage Learning.

Gopen, G. D. (2004). *The sense of structure: Writing from the reader's perspective* (1st ed.). Longman.

Graff, G., & Birkenstein, C. (2014). *They say/I say: The moves that matter in academic writing* (3rd ed.). W. W. Norton & Company.

Hacker, D., & Sommers, N. (2021). *A writer's reference* (10th ed.). Bedford/St. Martin's.

Halliday, M. A. K., & Hasan, R. (1976). *Cohesion in English*. Longman.

Johns, A. M. (1997). *Text, role, and context: Developing academic literacies*. Cambridge University Press.

Knoblauch, C. H., & Brannon, L. (1984). *Rhetorical traditions and the teaching of writing*. Boynton/Cook Publishers.

Kolln, M., & Gray, L. (2017). *Rhetorical grammar: Grammatical choices, rhetorical effects*. Pearson.

Kuriloff, P. C. (1996). What discourses have in common: Teaching the transaction between writer and reader. *College Composition and Communication, 47*(4), 485–501. https://doi.org/10.2307/358598

Lunsford, A. A. (2019). *EasyWriter* (7th ed.). Bedford/St. Martin's.

North, S. (2005). Disciplinary variation in the use of theme in undergraduate essays. *Applied Linguistics, 26*(3), 431–452. https://doi.org/10.1093/applin/ami023l

Rossen-Knill, D. F. (2011). Flow and the principle of relevance: Bringing our dynamic speaking knowledge to writing. *Journal of Teaching Writing, 26*(1), 39–67. https://journals.iupui.edu/index.php/teachingwriting/article/view/26270/24281

Rossen-Knill, D. F. (2013). Refining the given-new expectation for classroom use: A lesson in the importance of audience. *Journal of Teaching Writing, 28*(1), 21–51. https://journals.iupui.edu/index.php/teachingwriting/article/view/20717/20250

Smith, K. G., Girdharry, K., & Gallagher, C. W. (2021). Writing transfer, integration, and the need for the long view. *College Composition & Communication, 73*(1), 4–26. https://doi.org/10.58680/ccc202131585

Sommers, N. (1980). Revision strategies of student writers and experienced adult writers. *College Composition and Communication, 31*(4), 378–388. https://doi.org/10.2307/356588

Vande Kopple, W. (1989). *Clear and coherent prose*. Scott, Foresman and Company.

Williams, J. M. (1981). *Style: Ten lessons in clarity & grace*. Scott, Foresman and Company.

Williams, J. M. (2003). *Style: Ten lessons in clarity and grace* (7th ed.). Addison-Wesley Educational Publishers.

4 What Do Research Team Members Say?

So far, we have discussed the existing literature on flow (Chapter 1) and highlighted the voices and insights of students (Chapter 2) and instructors (Chapter 3) as they think about flow in writing. In Chapter 4, we turn the spotlight on ourselves as researchers. We first describe the research team's process for developing a rating system that evaluates flow in paragraphs written by students, collected as part of our larger study of voice-based and rhetorical grammar-based approaches to teaching flow in writing. That process resulted in a rating system that included both holistic and analytic scoring. The holistic approach rated paragraphs on a 7-point scale, with 7 corresponding to paragraphs with the greatest degree of flow. The analytic scoring focused on four elements of flow identified by the research team: *Coherence*, *Cohesion*, *Internal Sentence Fluency*, and *Information Management*. Each of these elements were rated on a 5-point scale, guided by anchors that described degrees of effectiveness.

In the next section, we relate the elements and anchors developed by our research team to the literature discussed in Chapter 1, offering connections between the research team's conception of flow and the perspectives represented in student-facing texts and the scholarly work informing these texts. We then provide analyses of inter-rater agreement on each of these elements, as well as agreement on an overall holistic rating of flow, and demonstrate that the reader's holistic sense of flow cannot be reduced to any one of these elements alone. We conclude with recommendations for how our rating system could be used as a pedagogical tool.

Developing the Rating System

As part of the larger study comparing the efficacy of voice-based and rhetorical grammar-based approaches to teaching flow in writing, we collected sample paragraphs from first and final drafts from each student who participated in the study. Each student was asked to mark in their final draft a particular paragraph in which they had applied the strategies they had learned for improving flow during revision. Those paragraphs, along with their first-draft counterparts, were what we planned to analyze in order to assess whether the

DOI: 10.4324/9781003459460-5
This chapter has been made available under a CC-BY-NC-ND 4.0 license.

lessons on flow had a measurable impact on students' writing. To do so, we needed to devise a rating system that would capture changes in flow across the first and final drafts. Given our educational focus, we wanted a descriptive rating system that might aid future instruction. In other words, we hoped to devise a rating system that would not only capture the relevant elements of flow but also provide useful concepts and language for instructors and students to discuss whether or not a piece of writing flows, why it flows, and how flow might be improved.

We began the process of developing a rating system by reading the literature and drawing on our backgrounds in our respective fields to determine if there were any existing rating systems that fit all team members' perspectives on flow, or if there were particulars of a rating system that we wanted to build on. Ultimately, we could not find an existing rating system that met our study goals. While automated computational systems for assessing coherence and/or cohesion do exist (e.g., Crossley et al., 2016; Graesser et al., 2004; Lapata & Barzilay, 2005), they lacked the descriptive qualities that would ultimately allow instructors and their students to discuss the extent to which their writing did flow or might flow better. We thus decided to create our own rating system.

Our goal in devising our rating system was to create a common language for writing scholars, students, and instructors to discuss flow across disciplines. Five of the authors of the present book participated in the initial development of the rating system. As noted earlier, our team brought multidisciplinary lenses to this project: English, linguistics, cognitive science, creative writing, biology, and psychology. We also had different levels of experience teaching first-year composition, ranging from two semesters to more than 10 years. Throughout the development process, we openly discussed expectations about flow from our past pedagogical and disciplinary training, our experiences as writers and readers, the models set by the top journals of our respective fields, and personal preferences. Our hope was that by making these implicit and field-specific biases explicit, we would identify underlying components of flow that are expected across disciplines. Finally, we drew on our general familiarity with undergraduate writing and the specific successes and challenges of undergraduate writers in our composition courses. The resulting rating system represents what constitutes flow from the perspective of a multidisciplinary research team.

Drawing on our different academic backgrounds and experiences as writers, we used a grounded theory approach (Corbin & Strauss, 1990; Saldaña, 2009) to capture our particular perspectives on flow. We began our process by individually reading a random selection of student paragraphs from the first data set, which included a mixture of first drafts and final drafts. As each of us read, we assigned overall holistic impressions to each paragraph (e.g., "this has excellent flow!" and "this started strong and then came apart"), along with specific descriptions of writing features and reactions that informed the holistic impressions. We then reviewed our first impressions over a series of weekly meetings. Although our holistic impressions generally aligned (i.e., different team members identified the same exemplar paragraphs for effective flow), our descriptions of what accounted for a particular degree of flow focused on different features of writing (e.g., punctuation, logical progression, and sound). We eventually began using a 7-point scale to capture our holistic impression of each paragraph. A score of 7 indicated that the paragraph *flows great*, a score of 4 indicated *typical flow* (among first-year undergraduate papers, based on our experience as teachers), and a score of 1 indicated *barely flows at all/messy/sloppy*. Within those three anchors, we found the 7-point scale offered us flexibility to capture subtle differences in overall flow (e.g., scores of 5 vs. 6 vs. 7) that were easy to identify but hard to articulate.

As different features emerged, we clustered related features and labeled them to form potential elements of flow. The initial set included six elements that captured the extent to which each element enabled the rater to work through the text easily. We characterized the focus of each element as follows:

- *Reading Ease*: how smoothly the reader is or is not led through the text
- *Coherence*: the degree of thematic unity across the paragraph
- *Information Management*: whether the reader received the needed information at the expected time
- *Internal Sentence Fluency*: the degree of fluency in wording or phrasing
- *Cohesion*: how well sentences fit together (e.g., the way "Lego® pieces" fit together as in Williams's [2003, p. 83], definition described in Chapter 1)
- *Deep and Surface Connections Between Ideas*: how well the signals in the text aligned with the conceptual links between the ideas in the text.

For these emerging elements, we began to assign ratings on a 5-point scale, where 5 reflected a paragraph that made especially effective use of the element and 1 reflected a paragraph for which that element actively interfered with its flow. We then tested these elements using an iterative process of reviewing paragraph flow and looking for patterns in our ratings. In this process, we found that our scores for *Reading Ease* were often similar to our holistic rating scores, and thus, we eliminated it as a separate individual element. The features in the element *Deep and Surface Connections* also appeared to be captured across several other elements, and so it was also eliminated. In the end, we were left with four elements representing distinct contributors to flow: *Cohesion*, the quality of connections between sentences; *Coherence*, the thematic unity of the paragraph; *Internal Sentence Fluency*, the fluidity of sound within sentences; and *Information Management*, the scope and order of information within the paragraph.

While these elements' general definitions did offer some initial description of flow, we determined that, by themselves, they were too abstract if ratings were to have instructional power. In fact, as noted in the literature review in

Chapter 1, coherence and cohesion have been frequently used to characterize flow, but not in consistent ways that everyone agrees on. If these elements of flow were to be the basis of a pedagogically useful and reliable rating system, we needed to characterize them more concretely. This led us to develop a set of anchors for each element of flow.

Initially, each anchor was minimally defined. However, as we used these anchors and discussed rating discrepancies across team members, we fleshed out the definitions. Within each element, a score of 5 meant that the writer's effective use of that element of flow improved the rater's comprehension or experience; a score of 4 meant that the rated element did not interfere with reading; and scores of 3, 2, and 1 meant that the element led, respectively, to minor, moderate, or major interruptions to the reading process.

We recognized that the rating system gave more weight to flow issues (focus of scores 1–3) than to flow having a neutral or positive effect (scores 4 and 5, respectively). We ultimately decided to keep this rating system because it had two benefits. First, it was difficult for members of our team to meaningfully and consistently distinguish good flow from excellent flow. Second, given that most first-year college writers have limited experience with academic or professional writing, we expected that most would have minor flow issues as they worked to communicate new concepts. Thus, we decided that simply getting to a point where flow "got out of the way" would be considered a positive milestone.

In Table 4.1, we describe each of the four elements of flow and the anchors that we used for rating.

Before we describe how we used this rating system, it's worth noting the ways in which our rating system does (and does not) capture the various perspectives on flow discussed in the literature review in Chapter 1. We begin with the first two elements in our rating system, *Coherence* and *Cohesion*, which we represented as two distinct concepts. In our system, *Coherence* applied across sentences and involved an overall theme, whereas *Cohesion* focused on the link between one sentence and another.

Coherence anchors focused on the rater's ability to identify a clear sense of a central unified topic and on how well the ideas across individual sentences formed a unified whole. Raters could assign the highest score for paragraphs in which they experienced sentences working together to create an overall theme or unity. By contrast, raters could assign lower scores when they had to work to find the paragraph's overall meaning or primary focus due to unexpected changes in focus or multiple unrelated focuses. In the lowest rated paragraphs, the rater would find it difficult to say what the paragraph was about. This concern with thematic unity in our *Coherence* anchors corresponds to the perspectives from classical rhetoric definitions of unity (e.g., Aristotle, ca. 350 B.C.E./1994), which focused on oneness and holding together primarily at the level of ideas, and is also in line with the idea of an organic whole that emerges through the writing process (Knoblauch & Brannon, 1984).

Table 4.1 Rating Scale for Elements of Flow

Rating Anchor	Elements of Flow			
	Coherence	Cohesion	Internal Sentence Fluency	Information Management
5 (Aids Reading)	A clear sense of unity (central focus or well-connected multiple topics), ideas fit together, glued together, well-connected pieces of information, message is very clear, signals work across paragraph to enhance unity.	Each sentence fits well with adjacent sentences. Signals enhance sentence-to-sentence connections. Through deep or surface-level connections or transitions, the reader is helped to relate one piece of information to the next.	Smooth, fluid sentences that carry the reader forward and help/enhance meaning. Sounds good in one's head or the reader is easily propelled forward.	Has the expected amount, scope, degree of specificity or generality, and order information, the reader is pulled forward by getting just the expected information at the expected time. Smooth narrative and/or logical progression leads the reader through text.
4 (No Interference)	Message (what it is saying—take home message) is clear, possibly a loose unity, ideas tied by broad topic or focus.	No need to pause to think between sentences, uninterrupted reading, easy to read/process, possibly an occasional odd fit between sentences that does not interrupt reading.	Sentences generally working to convey meaning, no clunkiness or awkward moments, no pausing to work out sentence.	The expected amount of information with the appropriate specificity is there, even though it might not show up right when the reader expects it.
3 (Minor Interruptions)	Occasional unexpected shift in focus, unclear/confused focus or message, uncertain emphasis.	Occasional break in sentence-to-sentence connection that causes readers to pause or re-read but does not significantly interfere with working out meaning. Signals (e.g., *however*, *but*, and *yet*) may, at times, be misaligned with content.	Occasional clunky, stilted, or awkward phrases or punctuation missteps that cause a brief pause.	Some expected information is missing or not sufficiently specified; occasional irrelevant or superfluous information that slows the reader down, a rambly moment, occasional logical gap, too much information presented in clause, sentence or paragraph (causes processing overload).

2 (Moderate Interruptions)	Significant unexpected changes in focus, unrelated focuses.	Significant disjunction or frequent disjunctions between sentences that make it difficult to understand how one sentence is related to the next. May interrupt meaning or cause re-reading. Frequent jumpiness or disconnected ideas or pieces of information. Signals in conflict with content.	Awkward phrases or punctuation missteps that cause serious pauses, lead the reader to be unsure about intended meaning, might need to stop to work out sentence meaning.	Might ramble a great deal, stream-of-consciousness, excessive information, or burdensome amounts of information, excessive repetition, expected information regularly not provided or not provided when expected, significant logical gap(s). Might be difficult to identify which information even should be expected.
1 (Major Interruptions)	Unclear/confused focus or message, difficult to say what paragraph is about.	Marked disconnection between sentences. Lack of clarity in deep or surface-level connections. Interferes with understanding the paragraph focus/message/point.	Confuses the reader to the point of not being able to extract meaning.	Significant problems with the amount or scope of information, degree of specificity or generality, order of information, and/or logical progressions; problems lead the reader to have difficulty working out the point of the paragraph.

Whereas our description of *Coherence* focused on the whole text, whether that be a whole paragraph, a whole essay, or potentially a larger whole, the anchors for *Cohesion* focused on sentence-to-sentence connections and the ways in which these connections did (or did not) help the rater connect one sentence's idea(s) to the adjacent sentence's idea(s). Raters could assign the highest score for *Cohesion* for paragraphs in which they were able to easily connect one sentence to the next. By contrast, raters could assign lower scores when they had to work to find connections from one sentence to the next due to signals (e.g., *however*, *but*, and *yet*) that were misaligned with the content, or significant disjunctions between sentences. In the lowest rated paragraphs, the rater would struggle to relate the meaning of one sentence to the next, with notable disconnection between sentences, such that the rater's ability to work out the paragraph's meaning was disrupted.

While we have just presented coherence and cohesion as two different concepts, not all scholars view it this way. As discussed in Chapter 1, coherence and cohesion are closely related concepts. In fact, they often end up being conflated with or subsuming each other, depending on the scholar's perspective. For example, Kolln and Gray (2017) defined cohesion as "the connection of sentences to one another, the flow of a text, and the ways in which a paragraph of separate sentences becomes a unified whole," a definition that seemed to locate qualities of coherence and cohesion under the term cohesion (p. 139). Likewise, Vande Kopple (1989) explicitly unified coherence and cohesion, in this case using the term "coherence" to cover what Kolln and Gray (2017) referred to as "cohesion":

> When I use the term *coherence*, I do so to describe prose in which nearly all the sentences have meaningful connections to sentences that appear both before and after them. The terms cohesion and cohesiveness would probably work just as well to describe such connections. But I use coherence to describe these connections and more.
>
> (p. 3)

In contrast to Kolln and Gray (2017), Vande Kopple (1989), and others who conflated or combined the two concepts, Williams (2003) not only distinguished cohesion from coherence but also explained the relationship between them:

- Think of cohesion as the experience of seeing pairs of sentences fit neatly together, the way Lego® pieces do.
- Think of coherence as the experience of recognizing what all of the sentences in a piece of writing add up to, the way lots of Lego® pieces add up to a building, bridge, or boat.

(p. 83)

In our rating system, the primary distinction between cohesion and coherence was the level at which they applied to the text: Cohesion was about sentence-to-sentence connection, while coherence was about the sense of unity of ideas across the whole paragraph. In this way, our rating system aligns most with the distinctions drawn by Williams (2003).

Our *Internal Sentence Fluency* element focused on the fluidity of sound within sentences, and the anchors for this element captured the sensory qualities of flow. Raters could give the highest scores when they felt propelled forward by smooth, fluid sentences that sounded good in their head. In contrast, lower ratings could be given when raters had a negative sensory experience, that is, when things such as clunkiness, awkward or stilted constructions, or punctuation missteps caused them to pause or re-read to work out a sentence's meaning. Raters could give the lowest score when reading was more deeply interrupted by sentences they could not make sense of. The emphasis on the sensory experience of flow in the anchors for *Internal Sentence Fluency* aligns especially well with the voice-based perspective of Peter Elbow (2012) in that the anchors emphasize how each sentence sounds in the reader's head.

In our anchors for *Internal Sentence Fluency*, we explicitly tied the sensory experience to sentence-level features, such as phrasing and punctuation choices to hold up the way these features might aid or interfere with the reader's ability to extract meaning from a sentence, as well as their felt experience while reading. Here, we can see a connection with Csikszentmihalyi's (1990) conception of a flow state, in which the individual experiences unimpeded concentration that leads them to lose track of time and their own conscious thought processes. The kinds of features that led to lower ratings for *Internal Sentence Fluency* were also those which resulted in disruptions to the state of unimpeded concentration. Anchors for lower scores mentioned the need to pause or even completely stop reading in order to work out the intended meaning of a sentence.

The *Information Management* element focused on the scope and order of information within the paragraph. As did the anchors for *Internal Sentence Fluency*, the anchors for *Information Management* highlighted the feeling of being led through a text. However, rather than focusing on aspects internal to sentences, this element focused on the arrangement of information with respect to readers' expectations for particular information at particular moments. Thus, ratings for this element depended on how information moved in and out of the reader's consciousness, an idea that was central to how Chafe (1994) framed flow.

The anchors we created for *Information Management* specifically referenced "reader expectations," such as those relating to cognitive schemas for organization (Flower & Hayes, 1980; Hartwell, 1979; Johns, 1997; Podis & Podis, 1990), or expectations of relevance (Grice, 1989; Rossen-Knill, 2011; Sperber & Wilson, 1995), as well as the work on questions under discussion

(QUD; Beaver et al., 2017; Larsson, 1996; Roberts, 2012). Raters could assign the highest score for *Information Management* when they felt that the paragraph's organization of information pulled them through the text; this involved getting only the information they expected in the expected amount, scope, degree of specificity or generality, and order. In contrast, raters could assign lower scores to paragraphs in cases where the expected information was missing or underspecified, where superfluous information was included, or where the amount of information presented caused the feeling of processing overload. Raters could give the lowest score to those paragraphs for which they struggled to work out the point of the paragraph due to the amount or scope of information, degree of specificity or generality, order of information, or logical progression.

Using textual signals to manage readers' expectations about information is a key function of metadiscourse. While the anchors do not explicitly mention metadiscourse, they do mention "signals" and/or "expectations," which point to the importance of metadiscourse to our elements. In the anchors for *Cohesion* and *Coherence*, there are numerous mentions of effective (or ineffective) uses of signals; these signals frequently took the form of words or phrases that show, as Vande Kopple (1989) said, how "parts of passages are connected to each other" (p. 56). These signals correspond to what Vande Kopple (1989) called "connectives" (p. 56), Williams (2003) termed "logical connections" (p. 66), and Graff and Birkenstein (2021) focused on in the chapter "'As a Result': *Connecting the Parts*" (p. 105). Though given different names, the various signals reflect the type of metadiscourse that is used to organize and guide the reader through a text.

One of metadiscourse's functions is to lead readers to expect particular kinds of information at certain points in the text. Not surprisingly, then, metadiscourse might also impact ratings for *Information Management*. Take, for example, the sentence, *I will next discuss the possible structures of metadiscourse*. If the next sentence is *Metadiscourse may be a phrase, a clause, or several sentences or paragraphs*, the reader will likely continue reading because they received the information the first sentence led them to expect. Consider, however, this next sequence of sentences: *I will next discuss the possible structures of metadiscourse. The lucky mouse was not caught by the cat*. Quite likely, a reader will stop reading somewhere in the middle of the second sentence because they did not get the information the first sentence led them to expect. These effective or ineffective uses of metadiscourse had a role in raters' perceptions of flow in relation to *Information Management*. For similar reasons, metadiscourse might also influence raters' sense of *Internal Sentence Fluency*.

As was clear in the literature review in Chapter 1, there is no single, simple way to define flow. Using the grounded theory approach described earlier, we arrived at a set of four elements, each of which related to one or more (typically not all) of the different perspectives discussed in our literature review.

This may reflect not only the complexity of flow as a concept and experience but perhaps also the multidisciplinary makeup of our research team. Crucially, as we will see in the following section, the raters' holistic experiences of flow could not be reduced to any one of the elements we identified, suggesting that the four elements together capture disparate, but related, contributors to flow in writing.

Using and Evaluating the Rating System

Our paragraph-rating team consisted of two of the authors who had contributed to the development of our rating system and two undergraduate research assistants who had not. This enabled us to explore how easily our system of anchors for the four elements of flow could be used by individuals outside of the team that developed them and the degree to which a team of raters could agree on their ratings for each of these aspects of flow. We followed a process in which each rater first read the paragraph once, assigned a holistic rating on a 7-point scale, and then re-read as necessary to assign a rating for each of the four categories described earlier. After completing each batch of paragraphs, we met as a group to discuss our ratings.

We began with a set of 117 paragraphs collected from students as part of our study. Of this set, 34 paragraphs were rated by all four raters, allowing us to examine the extent to which our raters agreed on each element of flow. We used two metrics to measure rater agreement: Cronbach's alpha and intraclass correlation.

The first metric, Cronbach's alpha, evaluates whether raters will make similar distinctions between paragraphs. Many research assessment tools are evaluated using Cronbach's alpha. An adequate Cronbach's alpha (defined as $\alpha > .70$ on a 0–1.00 scale) represents general agreement on concept between raters and suggests they are responding to a similar underlying quality, even though different raters might use different score ranges. For example, one rater might be harsh (primarily using the lower range), another might be generous (mainly using the higher range) and yet another might be conservative (mainly giving scores in the middle of the range). But if all raters use the higher scores in their respective ranges on the same paragraphs, then they would still receive a high Cronbach's alpha.

The second metric, intraclass correlation, evaluates whether different raters will give similar scores to the same paragraph. This more stringent metric is used for applied contexts such as interviews that result in a grade or diagnosis (e.g., contexts where fairness matters). Adequate intraclass correlations (defined as $> .60$ on a 0–1.00 scale) represent strict agreement on scores between raters and suggest a paragraph would receive the same rating no matter who rated it.

Our four raters demonstrated adequate Cronbach's alphas on the *Holistic* ($\alpha = .76$), *Internal Sentence Fluency* ($\alpha = .81$), and *Information Management*

($\alpha = .70$) rating scales. This would suggest those rating scales could be readily adopted for research use with as few as 2–4 raters. In contrast, Cronbach's alphas for *Coherence* ($\alpha = .57$) and *Cohesion* ($\alpha = .61$) were subthreshold, suggesting there was enough agreement for conceptual discussion, but we would likely need all four raters to code a larger volume of paragraphs to obtain reliable scores for research purposes. The lower agreement on these two particular elements is not surprising, given the lack of consensus over the precise definitions and distinctions between coherence and cohesion found in the literature (see Chapter 1). As noted, it is possible that with more raters, higher Cronbach's alphas could be achieved for *Coherence* and *Cohesion*, but it may also simply be impossible to fully draw a distinction between these two elements because the aspects of writing that contribute to sentence-to-sentence cohesion do, in the manner noted by both Kolln and Gray (2017) and Vande Kopple (1989), work to create the sense of unity that we associate with coherence. In any case, it is clear that raters made similar distinctions when offering a holistic rating for a paragraph's flow, as well as when rating a paragraph's *Internal Sentence Fluency* and *Information Management*, while there is more variability between raters for *Coherence* and *Cohesion*.

However, our four raters were unable to reach a sufficient level of intraclass correlation to demonstrate "strict agreement" on scores for any element. This suggests that while our raters might have all agreed, for example, that a given paragraph worked well in terms of how information was managed, they still differed on the precise rating given for *Information Management*. An interesting pattern in our data is that the "harsher" ratings tended to come from the two instructor raters, while the more "generous" ratings came from the two undergraduate writing fellow raters. This may reflect the fact that instructors are regularly called on to provide critical feedback on early drafts and evaluative grades on final drafts, whereas writing fellows only offer critical feedback, but never grades. It may also simply reflect a greater degree of experience on the part of the instructor raters, given their graduate-level training in pedagogy and subsequent teaching.

Based on this result, our rating system might be a useful feedback tool during the peer review process: The high Cronbach's alphas suggests that different readers will generally identify and agree on the same areas to work on, and the scores each reader gives may be the basis for a conversation about why a text is or isn't flowing for a particular reader. However, the insufficient intraclass correlations suggest that it would be inappropriate to use the scores as the basis of grading because different readers might penalize the same issue more or less than one another. If instructors do use this rating system for peer review activities or as the basis for their own feedback to students, we would encourage them to be especially cautious with *Coherence* ratings: As a group, the rating team had an especially challenging time reaching agreement when rating this element. This is likely due to limitations that arose from evaluating paragraphs in isolation, which deprived raters of information from other parts of the text that could have helped them assess thematic unity. Without the earlier paragraphs of the paper to provide context, raters were dependent only on their own preexisting knowledge of the topic when attempting to assess the coherence of the paragraph and may have been missing information that would have made the underlying theme of the paragraph more clear. As was noted in Chapter 1, content knowledge plays an important role for readers, and failure to understand key terminology being used can affect readers' perceptions about the flow of a paragraph (Beaufort, 2007). We remain optimistic that *Coherence* ratings will be easier to generate when examining a whole paper, but instructors may wish to specifically address this point when using this rating system in class.

The remaining paragraphs were rated by 1–2 raters each, allowing us to explore the strength of associations (correlations) between the ratings across all 117 paragraphs. Examining the associations between the four specific concepts, it was notable that *Coherence*, *Cohesion*, and *Internal Sentence Fluency* each showed stronger correlations with *Information Management* (r values fell between .38 and .45) than with one another. This would suggest that writers were more likely to create paragraphs that had effective coherence and cohesion, as well as sentences that were smooth to read, when they had paragraphs that included all the relevant information.

When examining the associations between all four elements and the *Holistic* flow ratings, we were pleased to find strong correlations (~.5 or higher). This would suggest that each of the four categories did effectively underlie our first impressions. But *Cohesion* had the strongest correlation with the *Holistic* rating ($r = .74$), suggesting that at the single paragraph level, cohesion had the strongest impact on our raters' visceral experiences of flow.

Convergences and Pedagogical Implications

Overall, the process of developing a rating system forced us to make the implicit ideas we each had about what constituted flow explicitly. And while it is not surprising that we did not achieve perfect agreement in our ratings, what is striking is that we were able to distill our intuitions about flow into a relatively small set of four elements, all of which, as described earlier, do have some basis in the existing literature relating to flow.

While flow may be a difficult concept to pin down and our experience developing the rating system certainly reflected that difficulty, the rating system offers a potential framework for instructors and students, one that captures distinct, yet correlated, elements that correspond to what readers experience as flow. As has become clear, our holistic sense of a paragraph's flow cannot be reduced to any one of these elements alone. Thus, if our rating system is to be used in classroom contexts, it would be useful to retain a holistic rating alongside a specific rating for each element to allow readers to articulate their particular perspectives on flow.

At the same time, by breaking the concept of flow into constituent elements, we can begin to demystify what we mean when we say a paragraph flows or does not flow. After all, if instructors' feedback on writing highlights areas that do not flow (much like the infamous "awk") but doesn't explain why, then it is hard for the writer to know where or how to begin to address flow problems. A paragraph that doesn't flow because of issues with internal sentence fluency almost certainly demands different revision strategies than one that doesn't flow because of issues with information management. Our four elements and their corresponding anchors provide what could be a shared set of reference points for instructors and students to talk about flow. Since our elements align with varied work on flow, it also provides a framework for introducing different conceptualizations to students. For instance, if an instructor notes that the flow issues in one student's writing relate to the features of *Internal Sentence Fluency*, whereas in another student's writing, the flow issues relate to *Cohesion*, the instructor could recommend a reading aloud strategy to the first student and a given-new exercise to the second student.

The rating system that we developed might also serve as the basis for discussions about how to address issues with flow—which will, of course, depend on where a writer is in developing their composition. If, for example, a writer were working on early drafts—and given the strong correlation between each element and the *Information Management* element—it might be sensible to begin by addressing information management (*Is there anything missing? Is there any irrelevant information?*) before working on other issues. This is, of course, in line with standard advice within rhetoric and composition to save sentence-level revisions until later in the process. After all, it may not make sense to begin working on features related to *Internal Sentence Fluency* by making changes to sentences that could end up being removed entirely because of information management issues. Similarly, it might be difficult to improve sentence-to-sentence *Cohesion* when an important piece of information is missing as a potential link. Of course, in order to decide what information actually is necessary, students will need to determine the central idea of their paragraph, a process that potentially improves the overall *Coherence* of their paragraph. Once information is solidly in place, students may wish to wrap up the process of addressing flow issues by focusing on *Cohesion* as this feature had the strongest link to raters' holistic experiences of flow.

It is important to note here that the four elements and their corresponding anchors, arising as they did through an extensive process based on grounded theory, are not simply restatements of any particular theoretical approach to thinking about flow. And yet, many of the perspectives discussed in Chapter 1 do seem to underlie the elements and anchors we arrived at through that process. The voice-based approach to thinking about flow (Elbow, 2012; Elbow & Belanoff, 2000) is reflected most obviously in our *Internal Sentence Fluency* anchors, while ideas about cohesion and coherence from Williams (2003), Kolln and Gray (2017), and Vande Kopple (1989) are, unsurprisingly, suggested in the anchors for *Cohesion* and *Coherence*. Our *Information Management* anchors reflect ideas about relevance (Grice, 1989; Sperber & Wilson, 1995; Rossen-Knill, 2011) and organizational strategies and schemas (Flower & Hayes, 1980; Hartwell, 1979; Johns, 1997; Podis & Podis, 1990), as well as work on QUD (Beaver et al., 2017; Larsson, 1996; Roberts, 2012).

What this suggests is that when it comes to helping students produce writing that flows well, a single lesson on flow rooted in a single theoretical perspective will not suffice. Instead, we can offer students a foundation that recognizes the multiple contributors to what we experience as flow in writing and help them identify strategies that can be used to sense, evaluate, and enhance the flow in their writing.

That our raters did not perfectly agree on their ratings for each of these elements suggests another important lesson: While we have identified a set of elements that contribute to flow, we have not suggested that readers will respond to these elements in the same way. If we have learned anything from working with a multidisciplinary team to identify key elements of flow, it is surely the opposite. Each reader is an individual and responds differently to the effects of different elements across different reading experiences. Of course, this brings us back to one of the most important practices for writers: finding and listening to different readers' experiences. Ideally, whenever possible, students interested in improving flow should seek out readers who reflect the intended audience. This is because not all readers are meant to read all pieces of writing, and as we discussed in Chapter 1, some readers may not be ideal readers for a particular text due to a lack of specific disciplinary, cultural, or situational knowledge. This means that as writers seek out readers for feedback specifically about flow, they should consider what their intended audience's disciplinary, cultural, and situational expectations might be and seek feedback on flow from readers who can offer insights from those perspectives. This is not to say that feedback from readers outside of those perspectives cannot be valuable. Indeed, it is often quite fruitful to seek out feedback from readers who do not share our knowledge and background. But if the goal is to improve the flow of a given text, feedback from those who closely resemble the intended readership for the text will be most valuable.

What is important is that we do not leave students to figure out the nebulous concept of flow on their own. Our rating system, with the four elements we've identified and the anchors developed for each of them, represents an approachable way to help students see and conceptualize the various elements that contribute to the felt sense of flow within a piece of writing, without necessarily needing to go into a deep dive into the theoretical underpinnings as we did in Chapter 1. The anchors for scores of 5 provide a description of what highly effective flow would look like in relation to each element, while the anchors for scores below 4 offer a picture of the various ways in which flow can break down. Drawing on the anchors for each element, instructors can design activities in which students use these elements to assess and address flow issues in their own writing. This approach ensures that flow concerns are not deprioritized while helping the student maintain ownership over their own writing.

References

Beaufort, A. (2007). *College writing and beyond: A new framework for university writing instruction.* Utah State University Press.
Beaver, D. I., Roberts, C., Simons, M., & Tonhauser, J. (2017). Questions under discussion: Where information structure meets projective content. *Annual Review of Linguistics, 3*, 265–284. https://doi.org/10.1146/annurev-linguistics-011516-033952
Chafe, W. (1994). *Discourse, consciousness, and time: The flow and displacement of conscious experience in speaking and writing.* University of Chicago Press.
Corbin, J. M., & Strauss, A. (1990). Grounded theory research: Procedures, canons, and evaluative criteria. *Qualitative Sociology, 13*(1), 3–21. https://doi.org/10.1007/BF00988593
Crossley, S. A., Kyle, K., & McNamara, D. S. (2016). The Tool for the Automatic Analysis of Text Cohesion (TAACO): Automatic assessment of local, global, and text cohesion. *Behavior Research Methods, 48*, 1227–1237. https://doi.org/10.3758/s13428-015-0651-7
Csikszentmihalyi, M. (1990). *Flow: The psychology of optimal experience* (1st ed.). Harper & Row.
Elbow, P. (2012). *Vernacular eloquence: What speech can bring to writing.* Oxford University Press.
Elbow, P., & Belanoff, P. (2000). *Sharing and responding* (3rd ed.). McGraw-Hill Higher Education.
Flower, L., & Hayes, J. R. (1980). The cognition of discovery: Defining a rhetorical problem. *College Composition and Communication, 31*(1), 21–32. https://doi.org/10.2307/356630
Graesser, A. C., McNamara, D. S., Louwerse, M. M., & Cai, Z. (2004). Coh-Metrix: Analysis of text on cohesion and language. *Behavior Research Methods, Instruments, & Computers, 36*(2), 193–202. https://doi.org/10.3758/BF03195564
Graff, G., & Birkenstein, C. (2021). *They say/I say: The moves that matter in academic writing* (5th ed.). W. W. Norton & Company.
Grice, P. (1989). *Studies in the way of words.* Harvard University Press. https://hdl.handle.net/2027/heb08428.0001.001
Hartwell, P. (1979). Teaching arrangement: A pedagogy. *College English, 40*(5), 548–554. https://doi.org/10.2307/376327
Johns, A. M. (1997). *Text, role, and context: Developing academic literacies.* Cambridge University Press.
Knoblauch, C. H., & Brannon, L. (1984). *Rhetorical traditions and the teaching of writing.* Boynton/Cook Publishers.
Kolln, M., & Gray, L. (2017). *Rhetorical grammar: Grammatical choices, rhetorical effects.* Pearson.

Lapata, M., & Barzilay, R. (2005). Automatic evaluation of text coherence: Models and representations. *IJCAI'05: Proceedings of the Nineteenth International Joint Conference on Artificial Intelligence, 19*, 1085–1090. www.ijcai.org/Proceedings/05/Papers/0505.pdf

Larsson, S. (1996). *Computing implicature: The case of relevance.* [Master's thesis, University of Göteborg]. https://citeseerx.ist.psu.edu/viewdoc/download?doi=10.1.1.592.6349&rep=rep1&type=pdf

Podis, J. M., & Podis, L. A. (1990). Identifying and teaching rhetorical plans for arrangement. *College Composition and Communication, 41*(4), 430–442. https://doi.org/10.2307/357932

Roberts, C. (2012). Information structure in discourse: Towards an integrated formal theory of pragmatics. *Semantics & Pragmatics, 5*, Article 6. https://doi.org/10.3765/sp.5.6

Rossen-Knill, D. (2011). Flow and the principle of relevance: Bringing our dynamic speaking knowledge to writing. *Journal of Teaching Writing, 26*(1), 39–67. https://journals.iupui.edu/index.php/teachingwriting/article/view/26270/24281

Saldaña, J. (2009). *The coding manual for qualitative researchers.* SAGE Publications.

Sperber, D., & Wilson, D. (1995). *Relevance: Communication and cognition* (2nd ed.). Blackwell Publishing.

Vande Kopple, W. (1989). *Clear and coherent prose.* Scott, Foresman and Company.

Williams, J. M. (2003). *Style: Ten lessons in clarity and grace* (7th ed.). Addison-Wesley Educational Publishers.

5 Conclusion
What Is Flow in Writing?

In writing, flow matters. Writers and readers feel this. But as scholars, students, and instructors know, it is not easily explained. In Chapters 1–4, we have heard multiple perspectives on flow in writing. As a whole, these varied voices create separate and, at times, harmonious melodies. We aim here to bring these voices together in order to provide a coherent way forward for teaching flow in the writing classroom.

Across student-facing texts and students' and instructors' comments, we repeatedly hear two broad approaches to creating flow in writing:

1) Critical to flow are conventional, decontextualized patterns, especially at the sentence level (e.g., parallel structure and transitions).
2) Critical to flow are the sensory experiences of the text (e.g., how it sounds).

This first approach harks back to classical rhetoric and its influence on early writing pedagogy, with an emphasis on "ritualized styles of speaking and writing," idealized models of text, and a "mechanistic, skill-based model of composition" (Knoblauch & Brannon, 1984, pp. 25, 80). In contrast, the second approach aligns with the idea that we can rely on our natural language abilities and senses to create flow (Elbow, 2012; Elbow & Belanoff, 2000). The first approach privileges structures over meaning, and the second approach privileges the writer's sensibility over structure.

These two approaches recognize the need to write effectively for an audience; however, the reader is not the primary concern. While instructors' and students' comments and student-facing handbooks and websites reference both structure and meaning, they do not explicitly relate the two. Nor do these resources hold up the primary role of the reader in creating meaning from the text, despite substantial pedagogical scholarship in these areas.

By contrast, the reader-focused literature discussed in Chapter 1 emphasizes the idea that flow depends on rhetorically situated patterns and expectations. It includes reader-focused strategies, such as schemas (e.g., Flower & Hayes, 1980; Hartwell, 1979; Johns, 1997; Podis & Podis, 1990), as well as strategies informed by systemic functional linguistics (e.g., Graff &

Birkenstein, 2010; Kolln & Gray, 2017; Vande Kopple, 1989; Williams, 2003) and the principle of relevance (Rossen-Knill, 2013; Rossen-Knill & Bakhmetyeva, 2011). These pedagogies share the view that writers and readers create meaning collaboratively. Moreover, they recognize that textual structure is inherently meaningful: It emerges from the needs and expectations of the rhetorical situation. While these meaningful patterns aid communication and do, to some extent, recognize general differences across discourse communities, they cannot account for each writer's and reader's unique background and how that might influence a particular writing and reading experience. However, these pedagogies have established an explicit and important connection between structural patterns and a sense of a unified, flowing whole. This is the territory of a third approach that emerges in the literature review:

3) Flow is co-constructed by the writer and the reader, both of whom depend on rhetorically situated patterns and expectations to create textual meaning (e.g., the performative nature of text, principle of relevance, questions under discussion [QUD], schemas, and rhetorical grammar).

While this third approach was not typically present in instructors' comments, students' comments, or student-facing texts, it emerged through the process of developing our rating scale. Our multidisciplinary research team voiced different perspectives on flow—a living and lively testament to our different backgrounds and experiences! Through our disagreements and agreements, we came to understand that the complexity of flow required separate but complementary perspectives. It required simultaneous attention to meaning as a whole and to the elements that make up this whole—ultimately the framework for our rating system.

Quite unlike the majority of perspectives among our study's instructors and students, and the popular student-facing handbooks and websites, our rating system does reflect the range of perspectives presented in the literature review in Chapter 1. As discussed in Chapter 4, a sensory voice-based approach (Elbow, 2012) can be felt in our *Internal Sentence Fluency* anchors. Linguistics-based ideas about cohesion and coherence (e.g., Kolln & Gray, 2017; Vande Kopple, 1989; Williams, 2003) align with our *Cohesion* and *Coherence* anchors. In addition, work in relevance (Grice, 1989; Sperber & Wilson, 1995) applied to writing instruction (Rossen-Knill, 2011; Rossen-Knill & Bakhmetyeva, 2011), as well as the work on QUD (Beaver et al., 2017; Larsson, 1996; Roberts, 2012), can be found in our *Information Management* anchors, as can ideas about organizational strategies and schemas (Flower & Hayes, 1980; Hartwell, 1979; Johns, 1997; Podis & Podis, 1990).

It is important to emphasize that each member of our research team brought unique perspectives shaped by natural tendencies, academic training in different areas, and a wide range of life experiences (academic and otherwise). As described in Chapter 4, we did not easily agree on a set of elements constituting flow. Furthermore, our raters did not perfectly agree on their ratings for each of the elements we did identify. This brings us again to one of the most important lessons from our research: Readers do not respond to these elements in the same way. In fact, quite the opposite was true. As readers, we responded differently to the effects of different elements across different reading experiences.

Our rating system, then, does not represent a single perspective on flow. Rather, it brings together four key elements that collectively represent the perspectives of writing scholars, students, instructors, and our research team. As we indicated strongly in Chapter 4, this rating system should not be used to score flow for the purposes of grading (our results indicate that it is not appropriate for this purpose), but rather as a basis for writers and readers to investigate, discuss, and create flow in writing.

Although the rating system does offer a basis for considering flow in writing, it would likely be most useful if grounded in coherent instruction that captures all three of the instructional approaches discussed before. As we learned from our study, there has been a need for an explicit and coherent description of flow in writing. Equally important, this description must capture not only the first two approaches based, respectively, on classical rhetoric and on the organic development of text but also the third reader-focused approach. That is, it should make clear that flow is co-constructed by the writer and the reader and thus depends on rhetorically situated patterns and expectations.

To this end, we include in the Appendix two sets of lesson plans for a full paper cycle in a college writing course. The first set of instructional materials, grounded in Peter Elbow's work, is voice-based.[1] It is highly performative, which is to say that it is a sensory approach that holds up the presence of readers and the writer–reader relationship. As such, it offers strategies not only for sensing one's work but also for performing it as a real act of communication. In contrast to the sensory approach, the second set of instructional materials is analytical. It draws on the principle of relevance and the given-new and end-focus principles from rhetorical grammar to offer linguistic knowledge that enables writers to make meaningful sentence-level choices and learn the effects of these choices on readers. Although these sets of materials clearly approach flow from different perspectives, they both address a critical need suggested by our study findings, that is, to create experiences for students that make real the situated nature of writing and reading and the reader's primary role in making meaning.

We understand both from our study and from our experiences that for many valid and varied reasons, some instructors will favor an organic sensory approach, whereas others will prefer the explanatory power of the analytical approach. This may lead some to take an either–or approach to flow instruction—sensory-based or analytical. It is also important to note that instructors often conflate the textual patterns of their discipline with more general concerns like flow. This rating system might help disambiguate the issues.

But, of course, our students—themselves readers—also bring their unique backgrounds and histories of experiences that shape their ability to learn in our classrooms. For their sake, we encourage instructors to try both the sensory and analytical approaches and to consider using them together. This mixed approach supports pedagogically inclusive teaching as well as accounting for the multiple elements of flow. To help instructors move toward this mixed approach, we include in the Appendix a limited set of resources, including student-facing texts that are particularly accessible.

While we have sought out and drawn on multiple perspectives to offer a coherent description of flow, we recognize that more work needs to be done to account for the diversity of writers, readers, and writing situations. Importantly, we do not consider our description of flow to be a static rubric or the final word. Rather, we view it as a tool that grounds and extends the conversation about what constitutes flow in writing. We view it as the basis for future research that might reveal how writers and readers from particular linguistic, educational, or cultural backgrounds identify different elements of flow or prioritize particular elements in different ways. For example, pedagogical studies might investigate the relationship between differences in linguistic or cultural backgrounds and a preference for a sensory or analytic approach to evaluating and improving flow.

Finally—as we use this moment of metadiscourse to signal this book's end—we realize that we are simultaneously hearing and feeling and seeing the text. And so we wonder, *how **does** each particular reader experience it?* This is how we have come to understand flow in writing, as a coherent multiplicity, a set of elements—discrete, complementary, and overlapping—that carry us through a text to create a thematic whole.

Note

1. We are especially grateful to Peter Elbow for reviewing these materials.

References

Beaver, D. I., Roberts, C., Simons, M., & Tonhauser, J. (2017). Questions under discussion: Where information structure meets projective content. *Annual Review of Linguistics*, *3*, 265–284. https://doi.org/10.1146/annurev-linguistics-011516-033952

Elbow, P. (2012). *Vernacular eloquence: What speech can bring to writing*. Oxford University Press.

Elbow, P., & Belanoff, P. (2000). *Sharing and responding* (3rd ed.). McGraw-Hill Higher Education.

Flower, L., & Hayes, J. R. (1980). The cognition of discovery: Defining a rhetorical problem. *College Composition and Communication*, *31*(1), 21–32. https://doi.org/10.2307/356630

Graff, G., & Birkenstein, C. (2010). *They say/I say: The moves that matter in academic writing* (2nd ed.). W. W. Norton & Company.

Grice, P. (1989). *Studies in the way of words*. Harvard University Press. https://hdl.handle.net/2027/heb08428.0001.001

Hartwell, P. (1979). Teaching arrangement: A pedagogy. *College English, 40*(5), 548–554. https://doi.org/10.2307/376327

Johns, A. M. (1997). *Text, role, and context: Developing academic literacies*. Cambridge University Press.

Knoblauch, C. H., & Brannon, L. (1984). *Rhetorical traditions and the teaching of writing*. Boynton/Cook Publishers.

Kolln, M., & Gray, L. (2017). *Rhetorical grammar: Grammatical choices, rhetorical effects*. Pearson.

Larsson, S. (1996). *Computing implicature: The case of relevance* [Master's thesis, University of Göteborg]. https://citeseerx.ist.psu.edu/viewdoc/download?doi=10.1.1.592.6349&rep=rep1&type=pdf

Podis, J. M., & Podis, L. A. (1990). Identifying and teaching rhetorical plans for arrangement. *College Composition and Communication, 41*(4), 430–442. https://doi.org/10.2307/357932

Roberts, C. (2012). Information structure: Towards an integrated formal theory of pragmatics. *Semantics & Pragmatics, 5*, 1–69. https://doi.org/10.3765/sp.5.6

Rossen-Knill, D. (2011). Flow and the principle of relevance: Bringing our dynamic speaking knowledge to writing. *Journal of Teaching Writing, 26*(1), 39–67. https://journals.iupui.edu/index.php/teachingwriting/article/view/26270/24281

Rossen-Knill, D. F. (2013). Refining the given-new expectation for classroom use: A lesson in the importance of audience. *Journal of Teaching Writing, 28*(1), 21–51. https://journals.iupui.edu/index.php/teachingwriting/article/view/20717/20250

Rossen-Knill, D. F., & Bakhmetyeva, T. (2011). *Including students in academic conversations: Principles and strategies for teaching theme-based writing courses across the disciplines*. Hampton Press.

Sperber, D., & Wilson, D. (1995). *Relevance: Communication and cognition* (2nd ed.). Blackwell Publishing.

Vande Kopple, W. (1989). *Clear and coherent prose*. Scott, Foresman and Company.

Williams, J. M. (2003). *Style: Ten lessons in clarity and grace* (7th ed.). Addison-Wesley Educational Publishers.

Appendix
Two Sets of Instructional Materials for Teaching Flow in Writing

Deborah F. Rossen-Knill, Katherine L. Schaefer, Matthew W. Bayne, Whitney Gegg-Harrison, Dev Crasta and Alessandra DiMauro

This appendix includes two sets of instructional activities for teaching flow in writing[1]: 1) a voice-based approach informed by Peter Elbow's work and reviewed by him and 2) an analytical approach based on rhetorical grammar and the principle of relevance. Each set of activities is designed to accompany a full paper cycle.

Rhetorical grammar strategies may be new to many instructors. For this reason, we provide at the end of this appendix "Additional Background Information." Instructors may decide to use this additional background material solely for themselves or as the basis for class handouts or slides, either as is or in some modified form. In the scaffolded activities, we begin with an explanation of key concepts that ground the work we ask students to do and invite instructors to share these explanations with their students.

Voice-Based Instructional Materials

Schedule for Voice-Based[2] Instruction on Flow

Class 1: Reflection on flow in writing and introducing reading aloud to hear and feel our writing voices (last 20–25 min of the class)

1. 5- to 10-min reflection asking students how they usually improve the flow in their writing.
2. 10- to 15-min introducing reading aloud, using Elbow's approach.

Homework 1: Practicing reading aloud—and reflecting

Class 2: Practice reading aloud to hear and feel what does and doesn't flow (~60 min)

1. In-class discussion to develop comfort reading aloud and a supportive reading community (~10 min)
2. In-class workshop to practice reading aloud (~20 min)

3. In-class workshop
   a. To hear what does and doesn't flow (~20 min)
   b. To begin revising (models Homework 2) (~5 min)

Homework 2: Reading aloud for revision

Class 3: Reading aloud to hear and revise your own writing (~30 min)
1. In-class: discuss and share homework (~10 min)
2. In-class workshop to practice reading aloud to revise (~20 min)

Homework 3: Revising problem passages in student's own writing

Class 4: Reading aloud to hear and revise student's own writing across paragraphs (~35 min)
1. Instructor introduces the concept and rationale (~5 min)
2. In pairs, students read aloud and note problem areas (~15 min per student)

Homework 4: Coincides with completing final draft, of course, paper
1. Finding and revising problem passages in student's own writing
2. Reflection on reading aloud to improve flow

Instructors should select passages from course readings. For an example of a passage revised for voice, see Elbow, 2012, pp. 223–224.

Class 1: Reflection on Flow in Writing and Reading Aloud to Hear and Feel Our Writing Voices (~25 Min at the End of the Class)

Reflection on Flow in Writing (5–10 Min)

During this paper cycle, we'll be focusing on flow or how the ideas and sentences in your writing fit together. To begin, I'd like to get a sense of what you know and think about flow in your writing.

1. When you think about your own academic writing, which of the following best describes the flow in your writing?

    _____ Ideas seem to work together, but sentences feel choppy or clunky.
    _____ Ideas don't seem to work together, but individual sentences flow well.
    _____ Ideas and sentences work well together.
    _____ Ideas and sentences are both problematic.

2. What, if anything, do you typically do to determine if your own writing is flowing well?

3. When you learn that your writing doesn't flow, what do you do to try to fix it?
4. What techniques have you been taught to improve the flow of your writing?
5. How confident do you feel in your ability to improve the flow of your writing?

NOT AT ALL   1   2   3   4   5   VERY

Introducing Reading Aloud Concept and Homework (10–15 Min)

I. Introduce reading aloud, using Peter Elbow's approach:

- What is our rationale for reading aloud? Elbow (2012) explains, "We can enlist the language activity most people find easiest, *speaking*, for the language activity most people find hardest, *writing*" (p. 139).

II. Distribute Homework 1 and introduce homework goals:

- Read aloud so that you can hear and feel your writing. "Read it slowly, read it lovingly, pay attention to how it feels" (Elbow, 2012, p. 221).
- Emphasize that this may feel odd, even embarrassing—but that it's also GREAT FUN and can make writing more enjoyable.

III. In the class, teacher models homework assignment:

- Instructor feigns embarrassment and mumbles, "This is embarrassing," and then reads as if reading to one's self—typically too quickly.
- Demonstrating greater courage and saying, "This is going to be fun," instructor reads the passage again—but takes twice as long, exaggerating a slow reading speed.
- Instructor performs the text again, with more confidence, more courage, and more enjoyment.

Homework 1: Practicing Reading Aloud—and Reflecting

Here's a thought to guide your writing: "We can enlist the language activity most people find easiest, *speaking*, for the language activity most people find hardest, *writing*" (Elbow, 2012, p. 139*)*.

Directions: Take a few minutes to practice performing your own reading aloud to another person, someone you feel really comfortable with. The idea is to shift into performance mode.

- First performance: Read the passage as you would normally read it (and time it).
- Second performance: You may feel odd or embarrassed, but tell yourself that you can do this and make it fun! Now read the passage again, but take twice as long.

- Third performance: Perform it once more for your audience as if you were on stage and wanted them to hear every word perfectly. Really have fun with this!

Reflection: Take a moment to write/reflect on how it feels to perform your passage? What did you notice?

Class 2 (Full Class): Practice Reading Aloud to Hear and Feel What Does and Doesn't Flow

In this full-day class, your students will practice reading aloud to a silent audience and then use reading aloud to hear what works and what doesn't work.

In-Class Discussion to Develop Comfort Reading Aloud and a Supportive Reading Community (10 Min)

Instructor facilitates discussion:

- Based on students' reflections from Homework 1, discuss how students and the instructor feel about reading aloud. Encourage students to share feelings of embarrassment. Shift into sharing ideas for increasing comfort around reading aloud—and having fun with it.
- Do a warm-up reading aloud exercise (recommended by Peter Elbow) to practice being embarrassed and having fun with it: instructors and students get into a circle, facing outward, and read aloud the following guiding thought. Say it TOO LOUDLY, then say it again in a way that feels wrong, and then once more in a way that feels right. Be embarrassed and have fun!

Here's a thought to guide your writing:

> Some critics and writers say that a set of words is not "realized" or "complete" until read out loud—that words on the page are like a play script or musical notes on a page, mere ingredients for the creation of the real thing, which is a performance.
>
> (Elbow & Belanoff, 2000, p. 13)

In-Class Workshop to Develop Skill at Reading Aloud to a Receptive but Silent Audience (20 Min)

Here's a thought to guide your writing: "The goal is to try to stop running away from the sound of your own voice—even revel in it" (Elbow, 2012, p. 221).

I. Instructor models both reading aloud and listening roles

The instructor should model both the performer and audience roles. Begin by modeling the performer, reading slowly to help the reader hear each word and phrase as the writer intended, and then ask a student to perform a text while the instructor models the listening audience. Modeling the audience's role is crucial as students typically don't have much experience with simply listening to and enjoying texts read aloud.

II. Instructor gives students directions for reading aloud activity:

NOTE: For this activity, instructors should select their own passages. For an example of a passage revised for voice, see Elbow, 2012, pp. 223–224.

- Take a few minutes to practice reading aloud.
- Ask your readers, "Would you please just listen and enjoy?" (Elbow & Belanoff, 2000, p. 7) and then perform your passage.
- Begin reading aloud:
  - First performance: Read the passage as you would normally read it (and time it).
  - Second performance: You may feel odd or embarrassed, but tell yourself that you can do this and make it fun! Now read the passage again, but take twice as long.
  - Third performance: Perform it once more for your audience as if you were on stage and wanted them to hear every word perfectly. Really have fun with this!

III. In-class workshop: Reading aloud to hear what works and doesn't work

This in-class activity involves hearing what works and what doesn't work and revising as needed.

Step 1 (15 min): Instructor introduces the concept of reading aloud to hear and feel what works and what doesn't work. Use the following handout to guide the in-class activity.

To give to students for in-class workshop (instructors should select their own passages; for an example of a passage revised for voice, see Elbow, 2012, pp. 223–224)

Here's a thought to guide your writing: "Reading aloud works best for revising when we read to live listeners" (Elbow, 2012, p. 220).

<u>**Directions:**</u> Each student should read the passage aloud at least twice to a silent, listening peer and underline any sentence that doesn't sound or

feel right. When reading aloud, follow Elbow's instructions as closely as possible:

> Read it slowly, read it lovingly, pay attention to how it feels. . . . Try another way to say this. See if you can say it so it feels good in your mouth and sounds right in your ear.
>
> (Elbow, 2012, p. 221)

Step 2 (5 min): Instructor passes out Homework 2 and then models the assignment by reading aloud different possibilities to a silent, listening audience. As Elbow says, "Intonation is the secret of the universe" (personal communication, October 25, 2016).

Homework 2: Reading Aloud for Revision

Here's a thought to guide your writing: "Reading aloud works best for revising when we read to live listeners" (Elbow, 2012, p. 220).

Directions: You should revise your passage from the class by reading aloud different possibilities to a silent, listening audience. For this exercise, you should follow Elbow's instructions as closely as possible, "Read it slowly, read it lovingly, pay attention to how it feels. . . . Try another way to say this. See if you can say it so it feels good in your mouth and sounds right in your ear" (Elbow, 2012, p. 221).

For this activity to work, you have to be able to find different alternatives, which can be hard. Here's how Elbow (2012) describes the process:

> Sometimes it's enough to grab and shake myself, as it were, and demand a solution. . . . This can work. But plenty of times it doesn't. My search for a solution is often more like solving an intellectual puzzle: *What are some ways I could rearrange these words and find others and still say what I want to say?* I have to start fiddling with the words in a brute random way. *What if I started with the final phrase? What different words could I use?* It's often a process of trial and error.
>
> (p. 229)

Once you've found a better version through reading aloud, you should write it down and bring it to share with the class.

Class 3: Reading Aloud to Hear and Revise Your Own Writing (30 Min)

In this class, your students will bring the "finding" and "revising" skills together in their own writing.

In-Class Discussion of Homework to Discuss How the Process Worked (10 Min)

Students share/perform their "problem" and "fixed" passages from the homework with peers and discuss how each passage feels.

In-Class Workshop to Practice Revising Through Reading Aloud (20 Min)

Students should work in pairs, allotting 10 min for each student to practice reading aloud. Each student should read a couple of paragraphs of their own draft to the silent peer audience to find a passage that doesn't feel or sound good. Stay with this passage—say it in different ways until "it feels good in your mouth and sounds right in your ear" (Elbow, 2012, p. 221).

Read and re-read alternate versions of the problem passage, paying attention to how it sounds to your ear and feels in your mouth and body. Perform it, Elbow (2012) would advise, so that the listener can feel and hear it as you feel and hear it (pp. 221–222). Once you've settled on a version you like, write it down.

For this activity to work, you have to be able to find different alternatives, which can be hard! Elbow (2012) suggests these questions to guide the process:

> *What are some ways I could rearrange these words and find others and still say what I want to say?* I have to start fiddling with the words in a brute random way. *What if I started with the final phrase? What different words could I use?* It's often a process of trial and error.
>
> (p. 229)

Once you've found a better version through reading aloud, write the revision in your paper and continue reading paragraphs aloud to find and revise problem passages.

Homework 3: Revising Problem Passages in Your Own Writing, Three Parts

Here's a thought to guide your writing: "When we read writing aloud, it increases our chance of noticing any mismatches or friction between the outer *physical* experience of *hearing the sound* of our words and the inner *mental* or *cognitive* experience of *feeling the meaning*" (Elbow, 2012, p. 238).

Directions:

Step 1: Read at least three paragraphs of your own draft to your silent peer audience. If you come to a part that doesn't feel or sound good, stay with it and read and re-read until it does and then revise.

Read and re-read alternate versions of the problem passage, paying attention to how it sounds to your ear and feels in your mouth and body. Once you've settled on a version you like, write it down.

For this activity to work, you have to be able to find different alternatives, which can be hard! Elbow (2012) suggests these questions to guide the process:

> *What are some ways I could rearrange these words and find others and still say what I want to say?* I have to start fiddling with the words in a brute random way. *What if I started with the final phrase? What different words could I use?* It's often a process of trial and error.
>
> (p. 229)

Once you've found a better version through reading aloud, revise your paper to include the new version. Continue reading paragraphs aloud to find and revise other problem areas.

Step 2: Now perform your revised paragraphs again to hear the text as a whole to appreciate the new versions. Read slowly so that your audience can understand each word perfectly without looking at the text—and enjoy your performance!

Step 3: Now perform it one more time: Feel the flow between sentences and across paragraphs and note anywhere the flow feels interrupted—either within or between sentences.

Class 4: Reading Aloud to Hear and Revise Your Own Writing Across Paragraphs (35 Min)

In this class, your students will bring the "finding" and "revising" skills together to revise across paragraphs.

In-Class Workshop: Reading Aloud to Recognize Organization and Transition Issues

I. **Instructor introduces the concept (5 min)**
   Why should we read aloud?

   > Reading aloud also helps us hear problems in the larger structures of overall organization. . . . As we follow the twists and turns of the micro-organization, we lose sight of the macro-organization; we can't see the forest for the trees. Even though reasoning and logic seem much more matters of analysis than hearing—more mind than body—nevertheless we can often *hear* a lapse in logic. That is, we can hear when the train leaves the tracks, whether they are organizational tracks or logical tracks.
   >
   > (Elbow, 2012, pp. 225–226)

Appendix 103

II. **Students read aloud (15 min per student, in groups of 2)**
Each individual student should read at least five paragraphs (in order) of their own draft to the silent peer audience and note places where they felt that "the train leaves the tracks."

Homework 4: Locating and Revising Problem Passages

In this homework, you will find and revise problem passages and reflect using voice strategies.

Here's a thought to guide your writing:

> Reading aloud also helps us hear problems in the larger structures of overall organization. . . . As we follow the twists and turns of the micro-organization we lose sight of the macro—organization; we can't see the forest for the trees. Even though reasoning and logic seem much more matters of analysis than hearing—more mind than body—nevertheless we can often *hear* a lapse in logic. That is, we can hear when the train leaves the tracks, whether they are organizational tracks or logical tracks.
>
> (Elbow, 2012, pp. 225–226)

Part I. Finding and Revising Problem Passages in Your Own Writing

Step 1: Read your essay aloud to your silent peer audience, focusing on shifts between major ideas and paragraphs. If you come to a part that doesn't feel or sound good, mark it.

When you feel a break in the flow of ideas, play with different alternatives:

- Does something need to be added, removed, or re-ordered? If so, think about how you might rearrange things. As Elbow (2012) says, "Even though the mouth and ear can find the problem all by themselves, the mouth and ear often cannot *fix* the problem without help from conscious thinking" (p. 229). Feel free to try completely new sentences.
- Read and re-read alternate versions of the problem area to hear and feel the flow of ideas across paragraphs. Once you've settled on a version you like, write it down.

To create flow, you have to be able to find different alternatives, which can be hard. Elbow (2012) offer these questions to guide the process:

> What are some ways I could rearrange these words and find others and still say what I want to say? I have to start fiddling with the words in a brute random way. What if I started with the final phrase? What different words could I use? It's often a process of trial and error.
>
> (p. 229)

Once you've found a better version through reading aloud, write the revision into your paper and continue reading aloud to find and revise problem areas.

Step 2: Now perform your paragraphs again to hear the text as a whole to appreciate the new version. Read slowly so that your audience can understand each word perfectly without looking at the text—and enjoy your performance! In the final draft that you turn in for a grade, note the page(s) you worked on and how you used the reading aloud strategies.

Part II. Reflection on Voice Strategies

Now that you have finished the final version of your paper, I'm interested in hearing about your work with flow, or how the ideas and sentences in your writing fit together.

I. Please circle the part of your paper where you've worked on flow.
II. Describe the process you used so that I can see how you arrived at the current version. (Note: You do not need to restrict yourself to this unit's "reading aloud" strategies; help me see what was particularly helpful to your work on flow.)

I'm also interested in hearing about how reading aloud may or may not have affected your work on flow in your writing.

1. How well were you able to use reading aloud to determine when the flow in your writing was or wasn't working?

    NOT AT ALL   1   2   3   4   5   VERY

2. How well were you able to use reading aloud to fix problems with flow in your writing?

    NOT AT ALL   1   2   3   4   5   VERY

3. How confident do you now feel in your ability to improve flow in your writing?

    NOT AT ALL   1   2   3   4   5   VERY

4. How likely would you be to use reading aloud again to improve flow in your writing?

    NOT AT ALL   1   2   3   4   5   VERY

5. What was particularly helpful about this strategy?
6. What would you suggest to make this strategy more effective?

Rhetorical Grammar Instructional Materials: Using Relevance, Given-New, and End-Focus to Improve Flow in Writing

Possible Schedule for Relevance, Given-New, and End-Focus During a Paper Cycle[3]

Class 1: Reflecting on typical approaches to improving flow and introducing the principle of relevance (last 20–25 min of the first class on flow)

1. Reflection asking students how they usually improve the flow in their writing (5–10 min)
2. Introduce principle of relevance and Homework 1 (10–15 min)

HW 1: Working in pairs, students practice with the principle of relevance; texts may be quite rough (not freewriting) or further along

Class 2: Reading aloud with sample text and students' own texts; texts may be very rough first drafts (but not freewriting) or further along in the process (~60 min)

1. In-class work with the principle of relevance (~25 min)
2. Introduce the principle of end-focus (~30 min)
3. Introduce homework (~5 min)

HW 2: Students work with end-focus in their own writing (students share with peers in a follow-up class if the class schedule has enough time for this)

Class 3: Working with the given-new expectation on texts that are further along in the drafting process (not freewriting or very rough drafts) (~30 min)

1. Introduce the given-new expectation (~10 min)
2. Model the homework in sample paragraphs and revise (~20 min)

HW 3: Students work with given-new in their own writing using texts that are further along in the drafting process. Ideally, students share with peers in class 4 if the class schedule permits.

Class 4: Seeing how the reader experiences given-new (~50 min)

1. Working in pairs, students identify given-new information in their partner's writing and discuss how well the writer anticipated the reader's response; texts should be further along in the drafting process (not freewriting or very rough drafts) (~40 min, 15–20 min per student)
2. Introduce homework (~10 min)

Homework 4: Coincides with completing final draft of the paper

1. Find and revise interruptions in flow in student's own writing
2. Reflect on using the principles of relevance, end-focus, and given-new to improve flow

Class 1: Reflection on Creating Flow in Writing and Introducing the Principles of Relevance, Given-New, and End-Focus

In-Class Reflection on Flow in Writing

Name: _____

During the next paper cycle, we'll be focusing on flow, or how the ideas and sentences in your writing fit together. To begin, I'd like to get a sense of what you know and think about flow in your writing.

1. When you think about your own academic writing, which of the following best describes the flow in your writing?

    _____ Ideas seem to work together, but sentences feel choppy or clunky.
    _____ Ideas don't seem to work together, but individual sentences flow well.
    _____ Ideas and sentences work well together.
    _____ Ideas and sentences are both problematic.

2. What, if anything, do you do now to determine if your own writing is flowing well?
3. When you learn that your writing doesn't flow, what do you do to try to fix it?
4. What techniques have you been taught to improve the flow of your writing?
5. How confident do you feel in your ability to improve the flow in your writing?

    NOT AT ALL   1   2   3   4   5   VERY

Introducing the Principle of Relevance and Homework 1 (~15 Min)

Instructional Context: For this paper cycle, the class begins by finding places where flow is interrupted and then uses students' intuition—that is, the principle of relevance—to improve flow. The class then moves on to using given-new and end-focus to improve flow.

Instructor Begins by Helping Students Experience the Principle of Relevance

Use one of the activities in the "Additional Materials" at the end of this appendix to help students feel their natural understanding of the principle of relevance.

Instructor Discusses How Students' Intuitive Reactions in the Previous Activity Are Based on the Principle of Relevance (Rossen-Knill, 2011)

<u>What did we learn from the experience?</u> "Saying" and "meaning" are not the same. (Grice, 1989). Miscommunication is a natural part of communication.

<u>Why does it matter?</u> Communicators expect "relevance" (Grice, 1989; Sperber & Wilson, 1995).

BUT—readers may discover a relevant meaning that is different from the writer's intended meaning.
AND—while readers will work quite hard to find relevance, they expect a payoff worthy of their effort.
AND—when we can't find relevance or have to put in unnecessary effort to figure out what someone means, we get stuck, even annoyed.

Essentially,

- the greater the value of the interpretation to the hearer, the stronger the relevance;
- the smaller the processing effort, the stronger the relevance.

What does the reader do? To minimize processing effort, they select the first relevant interpretation that comes to mind (Sperber & Wilson, 1995).

Instructor Discusses Why the Principles of Relevance and the Given-New and End-Focus Expectation Matter to Writers

- There's always a chance that the hearer or reader will work out an interpretation not intended by the writer.
- The writer's job, then, is to maximize the chances that the reader will work out the intended meaning, which involves minimizing unintended meanings.

At the most concrete level, these concepts enable writers to

- see how the reader experiences their text,
- use readers' natural speaking and listening abilities to reveal readers' expectations and find problems with flow, and
- use intuitions as native English speakers and/or use given-new and end-focus to address problems with flow.

Instructor introduces "Testing for Relevance" to test sentence-to-sentence flow

Testing for Relevance: The Three-Step Audience Response Process

The instructor selects a paragraph for this activity. Begin with the first sentence of the paragraph.

Step 1: Without revealing what comes next, the writer reads the sentence aloud. The audience writes down the first couple of questions that come to mind (or a statement about what they expect the next sentence to be about).
Step 2: The writer reads the next sentence aloud (or what might be called the *responding sentence*). The writer and audience discuss: Does the second sentence begin to address the audience expectations written down in Step 1?
Step 3: If you answered "yes" in Step 2, repeat the test, this time beginning with the last sentence you read.

If you answered "no" in Step 2, you have identified a flow problem. This tells you that you need to revise.

Instructor Introduces Homework Handout:

In Homework 1, students practice using the principle of relevance to learn where flow is and isn't working. Provide students with sample paragraphs. As students begin to learn how to use relevance to find flow, they may benefit most from working on the same paragraph so that they can compare and discuss where they experienced flow and where they did not. This allows them to see that flow depends on, among other things, the audience. This, in turn, helps them understand why it is imperative for writers to test their work on readers.

Homework 1: Practicing the Principle of Relevance

Here are a few thoughts to guide your writing:

- "Readers have a strong intuitive sense of paragraph flow, and perhaps an even stronger intuitive reaction to flow interrupted" (Rossen-Knill, 2011, p. 39).
- The principle of relevance: Each sentence raises questions for the reader. Readers expect the next sentence to begin to address them (Rossen-Knill, 2011, pp. 52–53).

Directions: This activity will involve you and another person; the other person need not be a member of the class. You will play the role of writer; the other person will be the reader. Follow the following steps, using the paragraph distributed in class.

Begin with the first sentence of the paragraph.

Step 1: Without revealing what comes next, the writer reads the sentence aloud. The audience writes down the first couple of questions that come to mind (or a statement about what you expect the next sentence to be about).

Step 2: The writer reads the next sentence aloud (or what might be called the *responding sentence*). The writer and reader discuss: Does the second sentence begin to address the audience expectations written down in Step 1? You're not looking for an exact match, just a close match—a sense that the responding sentence meets the expectations set up by the previous sentence. Remember that readers shouldn't have to work unnecessarily hard to find the writer's intended meaning.

Step 3: If you answered "yes" in Step 2, repeat the test, this time beginning with the last sentence you read.

If you answered "no" in Step 2, you have identified a flow problem.

Note places where flow worked particularly well and places where it did not work (no need to make changes to improve flow). Please bring your results to class.

Class 2: Testing for Flow and Revising Using Intuitions and the End-Focus Expectation

In this full-day class, students will revise their writing using the principle of relevance to test flow using their intuitions and a few guidelines. They will also learn about the end-focus expectation.

Here are a few thoughts to guide your writing:

- Both in reading and in conversation our language is loaded with expectations; we have a sense of direction about language. Although we may not know exactly what's coming next, when we hear it—or read it—we recognize if it's appropriate. It's when the ideas take an unexpected turn that the "awk" response can set in, when a passage fails to fit that expectation, that sense of appropriateness

(Kolln, 2007, p. 64)

- Readers appreciate optimal relevance; they determine if the effort they put into understanding the writer's text matches the worth of the message.

In-Class Work With the Principle of Relevance (25 Min)

Step 1: Share homework to see what students discovered about flow in the sample paragraphs; be aware that students may or may not identify the exact same flow problems. This is because audiences differ. This is a good opportunity to discuss why writers need readers and need to know their readers.

Step 2: Small group work: Students try to revise flow problems in the sample homework paragraph, guided by the following suggestions.

If there is a flow problem between two sentences, consider

- revising or deleting sentence 1,
- revising or deleting sentence 2,
- or inserting sentence(s) between sentences 1 and 2.

Repeat as needed.

Introducing End-Focus (See "Additional Background Information," I—V)

I. **Modeling the process for Homework 2, the instructor works through the 4-step process for revising for end-focus (15 min)**

Step 1: Highlight the most important information to you as a writer.
Step 2: Move the most important information to the end of the sentence. Don't worry if a sentence doesn't work. The next steps fix this.
Step 3: Read the sentence. Highlight words, word groups, and punctuation that now seem odd or out of place.
Step 4: Relocate, replace, or delete odd or out-of-place words and word groups; if needed, re-punctuate.

II. **Students test and revise for end-focus in one of their own paragraphs (15 min)**

Homework 2: More Practice With End-Focus

In homework 2, end-focus will help you discover the most important information in your own writing and then revise to convey this to your reader.

Here are a few thoughts to guide your writing:

- Writing works best when it meets readers' expectations (Kolln, 2007, p. 64).
- Readers appreciate optimal relevance; they determine if the effort they put into understanding the writer's text matches the worth of the message.

Directions: Using the following 4-step process to revise for end-focus, work through two paragraphs of your writing. Revise as needed.

Step 1: Highlight the most important information to you as a writer.

Step 2: Locate the most important information at the end of the sentence. Don't worry if a sentence doesn't work. The next steps fix this.
Step 3: Read the sentence. Highlight words, word groups, and punctuation that now seem odd or out of place.
Step 4: Relocate, replace, or delete odd or out-of-place words and word groups; if needed, re-punctuate.

Class 3: Introducing and Revising Using the Given-New Expectation (30 Min)

Introducing the Given-New Expectation

Here's a thought to guide your writing: "It is wonderfully intuitive: Given information should come before new information . . . this principle characterizes the normal, default order of information in both spoken and written texts" (Rossen-Knill, 2013, p. 21).

Step 1: Instructor works through given-new "Additional Background Information," VI—IX, with students.
Step 2: Modeling Homework 2, the instructor and students identify given and new information in a sample paragraph, note problems, and revise. A previous sample paragraph might be used, or the instructor can select their own paragraph in keeping with course readings and theme.

Homework 3: Working With the Given-New Expectation in Your Own Writing

Here's a thought to guide your writing: Readers expect given information before new information.

Overview: Begin by using the given-new test to see where your writing meets and doesn't meet the given-new expectation and then revise as needed to meet the given-new expectation.

Part I. Imagine that your audience is a peer in your writing class. Reading as if you are your peer audience, **bold the new information**; underline the given information.

To figure out whether information is given or new, imagine that you are the audience and answer two questions:

Step 1

A. Is the information stated in the previous text easy to work out?

    a. If you answered "**yes**," then the information is **given**.
    b. If you answered "**no**," then go on to question 2.

B. Is the information suggested by the previous text or the situation easy for the reader to work out and expected?
   a. If you answered "**yes**," then the information is **given**.
   b. If you answered "**no**," then the information is **new**.
C. Mark sentences that do not meet the given-new expectation.

Part II. Revise sentences as needed to meet the given-new expectation. It may help use steps 2–4 of the 4-step process for finding and revising for given-new:

Step 2: Move the given information before the new information. Don't worry if the sentence doesn't seem to work. The next steps fix this.
Step 3: Read the sentence. Highlight words, word groups, and punctuation that now seem odd or out of place.
Step 4: Relocate, replace, or delete odd or out-of-place words and word groups; if needed, re-punctuate.

Please bring your work to the class, as well as an unmarked original version of the paragraph you worked on.

Class 4: Practice With Given-New in Your Own Writing (20 Min)

In-Class Workshop to See How the Reader Experiences Given-New in the Writer's Paragraph

For this activity, students will partner with another student. Both students will bring their original paragraph and the version revised for given-new. To begin, both students give each other their original unmarked paragraph and their revised paragraph. They then identify the given and new information in each sentence in their peer's original and revised paragraphs. Finally, they compare to learn how well they, as writers, were able to imagine their reader's sense of which information was given and which was new. Students should then discuss any differences between the writer's sense of given-new and the reader's sense of given-new and make a revision plan to meet the reader's sense of given-new (15 min).

Homework 4 (Turn in With Final Paper)

In this homework, you will find and revise flow problems in your own writing and submit feedback and a reflection on the rhetorical grammar strategies used. Please turn this in with your final paper.

Appendix   113

Part I. Finding and Revising Problem Passages

For a page of your writing, use the principles of relevance, the given-new expectation, and/or the end-focus expectation to see how each sentence flows into the next. In the final draft that you turn in for a grade, note the page you worked on and which strategy(ies) you used. It will likely be more helpful and more fun to practice these strategies with a peer.

Part II. Student Post-Reflection on Rhetorical Grammar Strategies

Name: _____

Now that we're at the end of our paper cycle, I'm interested in hearing about your work with flow, or how the ideas and sentences in your writing fit together.

1. Please circle the part of your paper where you've worked on flow.
2. Describe the process you used so that I can see how you arrived at the current version. (Note: You do not need to restrict yourself to this unit's rhetorical grammar strategies; help me see what was particularly helpful to your work on flow.)

I'm also interested in hearing about how rhetorical grammar strategies may or may not have affected your work on flow in your writing.

3. How well were you able to use rhetorical grammar strategies to tell when the flow in your writing is or is not working?

   NOT AT ALL   1   2   3   4   5   VERY

4. How well were you able to use rhetorical grammar strategies to fix problems with flow in your writing?

   NOT AT ALL   1   2   3   4   5   VERY

5. How confident do you now feel in your ability to improve flow in your writing?

   NOT AT ALL   1   2   3   4   5   VERY

6. How likely would you be to use rhetorical grammar strategies to improve flow in your future writing?

   NOT AT ALL   1   2   3   4   5   VERY

7. What was particularly helpful about this strategy?
8. What would you suggest to make this strategy more effective?

Additional Materials

Activities That Help Students Feel the Principle of Relevance

Activity 1: Use the following "Do you want a cup of coffee?" example to help students see that as speakers and listeners, we are experts at using the principle of relevance to work out the possible meanings of what is said.

Part I. Feeling the Principle of Relevance as Speakers and Listeners

A. Have a student ask you, "Do you want a cup of coffee?"
B. Reply, "It's raining outside," and ask students what this means.
C. You are likely to get the following types of responses: *It means no or that the person might want a cup of coffee but not if it means going outside.*
D. Ask students how they knew what "It's raining outside" might mean. They may struggle with this, so you may need to help them see how people draw on the immediate situation to find relevance in what someone says. Communicators naturally expect and look for relevance (Sperber & Wilson, 1995).

Part II: Feeling a Problem With Relevance

A. Again, have a student ask you, "Do you want a cup of coffee?"
B. Reply, "The wall is yellow," and ask students what this means.
C. Students are likely to take longer to answer this or to have trouble finding a meaning. This is because it is *hard to find the relevance of the answer to the question.*
D. To transition to writing, explain that sentences in writing are in conversation with each other. This means that students can use their knowledge as speakers and listeners to feel when one sentence is not a relevant response to the previous sentence.

Activity 2: Use the following "It's cold in here" example to help students understand that what is said can mean many things and our intuitive sense of the principle of relevance—our expectation for relevance—leads us to work out different possible interpretations.

A. Write "It's cold in here" on the board and ask your students to write down what this could mean and encourage creativity.
B. Ask each student to share what they wrote down. You are likely to get the following types of responses: *The room is cold, I feel cold*, and so on. After a few such answers, you can encourage more unexpected meanings. Students may begin to offer such interpretations as *Please close the window, that's a mean person*, and so on, but they may not.

C. If students have not moved far from the literal meaning of "It's cold in here," ask if it might mean, *You forgot my sweater*, said by one member of a couple to another. Then provide the situation that warrants interpreting "It's cold in here" as *You forgot my sweater*.

Activity 3: Use the following "The dog is up" examples to help students understand that what is said can mean many things and our intuitive sense of the principle of relevance—our expectation for relevance—leads us to work out different possible interpretations. As context changes, interpretation changes. Without a shared focus on a particular context, writers and readers may come to different first interpretations of what is said.

A. Follow the same process as in 3A—3C. For 3C, if students have not moved far from the literal meaning, offer this possible meaning: *you'd better put your hamster away before the dog eats it* (said by a parent to a child who has the hamster out of the cage), or *my husband is up* (said by one woman to another after hearing the click of a beer can being opened).

Additional Background Information for the Rhetorical Grammar Approach to Teaching Flow in Writing

Additional Background Information on the End-Focus and Given-New Expectations

I. Introducing the End-Focus Expectation: Location Matters

Consider these three underlined information units:

<u>John</u>
<u>though typically known for his ability to focus under stress</u>
<u>could not focus</u>

How the writer orders information units tells the reader which information is the most important.

II. The End-Focus Expectation: Readers Expect to Find the Most Important Information <u>at the End of a Sentence</u>

Readers react strongly to end-focus. Which would you like said about you: A or B?

A. The writer writes: Jo has great soccer skills, but is slow.
 (Hmmm, slow, not sure we want them on the team.)
B. The writer writes: Jo is slow, but has great soccer skills. (Great skills, yeah, maybe we'll add them to the team.)

III. How Does Order Affect Meaning?

How the writer orders information units tells the reader what information is the most important.

1. John
2. though typically known for his ability to focus under stress
3. could not focus

According to the end-focus principle, "could not focus" is the most important information. Here's a full sentence that corresponds to this order: John, though typically known for his ability to focus under stress, could not focus.

1. John
2. could not focus
3. though typically known for his ability to focus under stress

According to the end-focus principle, "though typically known for his ability to focus under stress" is the most important information. Here's a full sentence that corresponds to this order: John could not focus, though he was typically known for his ability to focus under stress.

1. Though typically known for his ability to focus under stress
2. could not focus
3. John

According to the end-focus principle, "John" is the most important information. Here's a sentence that corresponds to this order: Though typically known for his ability to focus under stress, focusing was now difficult for John.

IV. How to Use End-Focus Across Sentences to Help Readers Find the Most Important Information? (Example Taken From a Student Research Paper)

Step 1: Mark the most important information to you as a writer (in bold face in this example).
A man leaves his house around 2:25 am. Just as he leaves his driveway, he **drives into a fire hydrant and crashes into a tree**. At the scene of the crash, **alcohol was not considered to be a factor**. The authorities decided to investigate the event further and many **shocking truths** were revealed. These shocking truths were made public and **this man's image was shattered**. Who was this man? Is he an ordinary, **everyday man who has a family**, or is he **a high-powered executive** at a major business? The story could be **about anybody**. Why was this story **the headlines on all the**

newspapers the following day? The answer to this question is a single person: **Tiger Woods**. Tiger Woods, the beloved professional golfer, was the man who **drove his car into a tree**. Tiger Woods was the man whose **life was changed forever that night**.
If the writer, Jae, is having difficulty finding the most important information, use **MAP** to analyze the text's message, audience, and purpose.
Message: Jae wants to talk about how Tiger Woods's accident changed his life.
Audience: Jae is writing to some of his friends, young college students who seek out excitement and adventure—sometimes without considering the consequences.
Purpose: Jae wants his friends to see that bad decisions can even bring down the rich and famous. His purpose is to convince his friends to make better decisions.

According to Jae's MAP, the most important phrases and clauses will present Tiger Woods as a successful person and relate his tragedy to the average person.

Step 2: Locate the most important information at the end of the sentence. Don't worry right now if a sentence doesn't work. The next steps fix this.
around 2:25 am **A man leaves his house**. Just as he leaves his driveway, he **drives into a fire hydrant and crashes into a tree** At the scene of the crash, **alcohol was not considered to be a factor**. The authorities decided to investigate the event further and many were revealed **shocking truths**. These shocking truths were made public and this **man's image was shattered**. Who was this man? Is he an ordinary, **everyday man who has a family**, or is he at **a major business a high-powered executive**? The story could be **about anybody**. Why was this story the following day the **headlines on all the newspapers**? The answer to this question is a single person: **Tiger Woods**. Tiger Woods, the beloved professional golfer, was the man who **drove his car into a tree**. Tiger Woods was the man whose that night **life was changed forever**.

Step 3: Read the paragraph. Mark words, word groups, and punctuation that now seem odd or out of place (underlined here).
a̲round 2:25 am A̲ man leaves his house. Just as he leaves his driveway, he drives into a fire hydrant and crashes into a tree. At the scene of the crash, alcohol was not considered to be a factor. The authorities decided to investigate the event further and <u>many were revealed</u> shocking truths. These shocking truths were made public and this man's image was shattered. Who was this man? Is he an ordinary, everyday man who has a family, or is he <u>at a major business</u> a high-powered executive? The story could be about anybody. Why was this story the following day the headlines on all the newspapers? The answer to this question is a single person: Tiger

Woods. Tiger Woods, the beloved professional golfer, was the man who drove his car into a tree. Tiger Woods was the man whose <u>that night</u> life was changed forever.

Step 4: Relocate, replace, or delete out-of-place words and word groups; if needed, re-punctuate. The paragraph revised for end-focus now reads:

Around 2:25 am, a man leaves his house. Just as he leaves his driveway, he drives into a fire hydrant and crashes into a tree. At the scene of the crash, alcohol was not considered to be a factor. The authorities decided to investigate the event further and discovered many shocking truths. These shocking truths were made public and this man's image was shattered. Who was this man? Is he an ordinary, everyday man who has a family, or is he a high-powered executive? The story could be about anybody. Why was this story the headlines on all the newspapers? The answer to this question is a single person: Tiger Woods. Tiger Woods, the beloved professional golfer, was the man who drove his car into a tree. Tiger Woods was the man whose life was changed forever.

V. In Sum: How to Use the End-Focus Expectation in Sentences to Help Readers Find the Most Important Information?

Step 1: Highlight the most important information to you as a writer.

Step 2: Locate the most important information at the end of the sentence. Don't worry if a sentence doesn't work. The next steps fix this.

Step 3: Read the sentence. Highlight words, word groups, and punctuation that now seem odd or out of place.

Step 4: Relocate, replace, or delete odd or out-of-place words and word groups; if needed, re-punctuate.

It's important to note that revising for end-focus will not address all of a text's issues, but it will improve flow and help the writer convey to the reader which information is most important.

The given-new expectation also improves flow and helps the writer convey their meaning to the reader.

VI. The Given-New Expectation: Readers Expect Given Information Before New Information

Readers expect given information before new information. "Given" refers to information or ideas that have already been established for the reader. "New" refers to information or ideas that are new to the reader. Readers follow your meaning more easily when given information comes before new information. Beginning with new information can confuse readers and cause them to stop reading or re-read in order to understand your text.

The next example and explanation show how the given-new expectation works. <u>Given material is underlined;</u> **new material (including in the title) is bolded.**

Sarah and the Yellow Apple

<u>Sarah</u> **went to the store to buy some apples.** <u>On the way to the store,</u> **she found a penny.** <u>She</u> **picked it up and put it in her pocket.**

Sentence 1 begins with "Sarah," which is given information that has been established in the title, "Sarah and the Yellow Apple." The sentence ends with new information, "went to the store to buy some apples."

Sentence 2 begins with "On the way to the store," which is given because it refers to the trip to the store that was established in the first sentence. The sentence ends with new information, "she found a penny."

Sentence 3 begins with the pronoun "she," which is given because it refers to "she" in the previous sentence and "Sarah" in the first sentence. The sentence ends with the new information about what Sarah did with the penny: "picked it up and put it in her pocket."

VII. To Figure out Whether Information Is Given or New, Answer Two Questions, Imagining That You Are the Reader:

1. Is the information stated in the previous text easy to work out?

    a. If you answered "yes," then the information is given.
    b. If you answered "no," then go on to question 2.

2. Is the information suggested by the previous text or the situation easy for the reader to work out and expected?

    a. If you answered "yes," then the information is given.
    b. If you answered "no," then the information is new.

VIII. How to Use the Given-New Expectation?

Step 1: **Highlight/bold the new information.** <u>Underline the given information.</u>

(For this exercise, assume that the information in the first sentence is all new and focus on the second sentence. Your question: which information in sentence 2 is new to the reader?)

Animal rights protesters called for a ban against dissection as a means to teach anatomy. **Computer programs can give students a sufficiently realistic and detailed representation of animal anatomy,** <u>they argued.</u>

The writer decides that "computer programs can give students a sufficiently realistic and detailed representation of animal anatomy" is new because it has not been established for the reader in the previous text or by the situation.

The writer decides that "they" is given because it refers to the "[a]nimal rights protesters" in sentence 1. The writer also decides that "argued" is given, because it is suggested in sentence 1 by "called for a ban," a verbal action that is typically associated with argument.

Step 2: Move the given information before the new information. Don't worry right now if a sentence doesn't work. The next steps fix this.

Animal rights protesters called for a ban against dissection as a means to teach anatomy. they argued **Computer programs can give students a sufficiently realistic and detailed representation of animal anatomy**.

Step 3: Read the sentence. Mark words, word groups, and punctuation that now seem odd or out of place (underlined in example).

Animal rights protesters called for a ban against dissection as a means to teach anatomy. they argued Computer programs can give students a sufficiently realistic and detailed representation of animal anatomy.

Step 4: Relocate, replace, or delete out-of-place words and word groups; if needed, re-punctuate.

Revised to meet the given-new expectation:

Animal rights protesters called for a ban against dissection as a means to teach anatomy. They argued that computer programs can give students a sufficiently realistic and detailed representation of animal anatomy.

IX. In Sum: How to Revise Using the Given-New Expectation?

Step 1: **Highlight/bold the new information.** Underline the given information.
Step 2: Locate the given information before the new information. Don't worry if the sentence doesn't seem to work. The next steps fix this.
Step 3: Read the sentence. Highlight words, word groups, and punctuation that now seem odd or out of place.
Step 4: Relocate, replace, or delete odd or out-of-place words and word groups; if needed, re-punctuate.

References

Elbow, P. (2012). *Vernacular eloquence: What speech can bring to writing.* Oxford University Press.

Elbow, P., & Belanoff, P. (2000). *Sharing and responding* (3rd ed.). McGraw-Hill Higher Education.

Grice, P. (1989). *Studies in the way of words*. Harvard University Press. https://hdl.handle.net/2027/heb08428.0001.001

Kolln, M. (2007). *Rhetorical grammar: Grammatical choices, rhetorical effects* (5th ed.). Pearson Education.

Rossen-Knill, D. F. (2011). Flow and the principle of relevance: Bringing our dynamic speaking knowledge to writing. *Journal of Teaching Writing*, *26*(1), 39–67. https://journals.iupui.edu/index.php/teachingwriting/article/view/26270/24281

Rossen-Knill, D. F. (2013). Refining the given-new expectation for classroom use: A lesson in the importance of audience. *Journal of Teaching Writing*, *28*(1), 21–51. https://journals.iupui.edu/index.php/teachingwriting/article/view/20717/20250

Rossen-Knill, D. F., & Bakhmetyeva, T. (2011). *Including students in academic conversations: Principles and strategies for teaching theme-based writing courses across the disciplines*. Hampton Press.

Sperber, D., & Wilson, D. (1995). *Relevance: Communication and cognition* (2nd ed.). Blackwell Publishing.

Notes

1. These materials are slightly updated versions from our mixed-method study of voice and rhetorical grammar approaches to teaching flow in writing, a study conducted in writing courses at two small private liberal arts colleges in the Northeastern United States.
2. Draws on the work of Peter Elbow. Special thanks to Peter for reviewing and approving these materials.
3. The Rhetorical Grammar Instructional Materials and the Additional Materials use and adapt material on the principle of relevance from Rossen-Knill and Bakhmetyeva (2011, pp. 122–131) and Rossen-Knill (2011), material on given-new and end-focus from Rossen-Knill and Bakhmetyeva (2011, pp. 176–183), and material on given-new from Rossen-Knill (2013).

Index

Academic Writing for Graduate Students (Swales & Feak) 24, 33
American Scientist (magazine) 33
Amis, Martin 18
analytical approach 34–35, 53, 92–93, 95; *see also* rhetorical grammar
Anson, C. M. 29
Aristotle 7, 12–13, 50, 71
audience(s) 6, 10, 11, 27, 60, 61, 90; awareness 47–49, 55–57; expectations 87; imagined 8; perspective 50; *see also* readers
"Audience Addressed/Audience Invoked" (Ede & Lunsford) 6
Aull, L. 11, 22, 24, 25
Austin, J. L. 21
authors' methodology 1–2; grounded theory approach 75–76; instructor perspective surveys 65–67; literature review 4; rating system for research team 74–83; student perspectives and coding team 43–49

Bahktin, Mikhail 8
Birkenstein, C. 12, 15, 26–27, 28, 68, 82
Bizup, J. 30–31
Bleich, D. 34
Booth, W. C. 13, 14, 21
Brannon, L. 6, 7
bridges, logical and verbal 32; *see also* transitions
Brief Penguin Handbook, The (Faigley) 57
Burke, Kenneth 5, 8

Chafe, W. 8, 81
Chaplin, M. T. 7
Cicero 5
classical rhetoric 5, 90; *Poetics* (Aristotle) 7
Clear and Coherent Prose (Vande Kopple) 12, 16, 22–23
coherence and cohesion 12–16, 21, 29; in rating system for research team 76, 77, 80–81
Cohesion in English (Halliday & Hasan) 14–15
College Composition and Communication (journal) 22
comment 17, 18, 22–23, 47–48, 49–51, 52–54, 57–59, 60, 66, 67, 69, 71, 90, 91
connectors *see* transitions
content knowledge 10, 85
cooperative principle 20–21
Corbin, J. M. 44
Craft of Research, The (Williams et al.) 27
Csikszentmihalyi, M. 9, 68, 81
culture-based textual patterns 10–11

Deaf community 35
dialogic process 8
Discourse, Consciousness, and Time (Chafe) 8
discourse studies 11

ear-based approaches 34–35; *see also* voice-based approach
EasyWriter (Lunsford) 29
Ede, L. 6

Elbow, Peter: on defining flow 3; on idea development 50; internal sentence fluency 81; on senses, role of 54, 71; on trial and error 34; *Vernacular Eloquence* 7, 55; voice-based approach 1, 57, 65, 68, 92; *Writing With Power* 7; *see also* voice-based approach
Elements of Style, The (Strunk & White) 28
end-focus 17, 19, 33, 48, 53, 70, 92, 105–107, 109–110, 113, 115–116, 118
English as Second Language 24
equity and inclusion 34
Everyday Writer, The (Lunsford) 28, 57–58
Exploring Grammar Through Texts (Paraskevas) 16

Faigley, L. 57
Feak, C. B. 24, 33
Fish, S. 28
flow: definitions 3–4, 71; impact and importance 90–91; rating system 75–76
Flower, Linda 8–9, 71
Flow in Scholarly Writing (handout; Purdue OWL) 31
flow in writing, literature review: coherence and cohesion 12–16; linguistics-based pedagogies 11–27; metadiscourse 22–27; pragmatics and language philosophy 20–22; reader-focused pedagogies 7–11; rhetorical approaches 5–6; rhetorical grammar 16–20; student resources 27–35; writer-focused pedagogies 6–7
fluency, internal sentence 76, 81, 86–87
form, metaphors for 7
functional grammar 11, 59

given-new (known-before-new / old-before-new) 17–19, 27, 31, 33, 34, 48, 70, 86, 92, 105–107, 111–113, 115, 118–119, 120

Glenn, C. 29
Gopen, George 19, 33, 68, 70
graduate-level textbooks 33
Graff, G. 12, 15, 26–27, 28, 68, 82
grammar *see* rhetorical grammar
Gray, L. 15, 16, 19, 29, 65, 80, 86
Gregory, M. W. 13, 14, 21
Grice, P. 20, 21

Hacker, D. 28, 29
Halliday, M. A. K. 14–15, 17, 18, 19, 33, 65
Halliday's Introduction to Functional Grammar (Halliday & Matthiessen) 17
Hancock, C. 16, 59
Harper and Row Rhetoric, The (Booth & Gregory) 13, 14
Harris, Joseph 21
Hartwell, P. 9
Hasan, R. 14–15, 19, 33, 65
Hayes, J. R. 9
Hodges Harbrace Handbook, The (Glenn & Gray) 29
Hofmann, A. H. 33
How to Do Things With Words (Austin) 21
How to Write a Sentence (Fish) 28
Hyland, K. 22, 24–25, 26–27

ideas, student perspectives on 49–52
information management 81–82
instructor perspectives 65–72
internal sentence fluency 81
Introduction to Functional Grammar, An (Halliday) 17

Johns, A. M. 9

Kaplan, Robert E. 10
Knoblauch, C. H. 6, 7
Kolln, Martha 12, 15, 16, 17, 19, 65, 80, 86
Kopple, Vande 12, 15–16, 18, 22–23, 24, 25–27, 69, 80, 82, 86
Kuriloff, Peshe 25

Lancaster, C. I. 22, 24, 25, 34
language philosophy and pragmatics 20–22

Lego® model of cohesion 14, 16, 76, 80
Leki, I. 10
Letter from a Birmingham Jail (King) 15
linguistics: linguistics-based pedagogies 4, 11–27, 71; systemic functional linguistics 14, 16, 17, 19, 59, 90–91
linking words 71; *see also* transitions
logical connections 23, 27, 82
Longman Handbook for Writers and Readers (Schwegler & Anson) 29
Lunsford, A. A. 6, 28, 29, 57–58

Markels, R. B. 50
Martin, J. R. 17, 18
Matthiessen, C. M. 17, 18
Meaning-Centered Grammar (Hancock) 16
meaning-making: and language 11–12, 17, 21; by readers 5–6; shared 12; by writers 5–6
metacommentary 26
metadiscourse 22–27, 82; markers 24–25; students' lack of awareness of 58–59
"Metadiscourse in Academic Writing: A Reappraisal" (Hyland & Tse) 24
Metzger, S. 22
Miller, C. R. 9
modern rhetoric 5–8, 12
Music of Form, The (Elbow) 54

On Paragraphs (handout; Purdue OWL) 32
On Writing Well (Zinsser) 28
organization, student perspectives on 52–55

Paragraph Organization and Flow (handout; Purdue OWL) 31
Paraskevas, C. C. 16
Podis, J. M. 9, 54
Podis, L. A. 9, 54

Poetics (Aristotle) 7
popular style books and writing handbooks 28–29
pragmatics and language philosophy 20–22
principle of relevance 21, 43, 48, 91, 92, 95, 105–109, 114–115
Problem-Solving Strategies for Writing (Flower) 8
process-based pedagogy 6–7, 59
punctuation 44–45, 59, 81
Purdue Online Writing Lab (OWL) 31–32

questions under discussion (QUD) model 21, 81–82, 87

Rawlins, J. 22
readers: as active participants 8–9; in partnership with writers 4–5; reader-focused pedagogies 7–11; *see also* audiences
reading aloud 55, 100–101, 102–103
relevance, principle of 21, 91; instructional sample 105–115
research team perspectives 74–88
Revising for Cohesion and Paragraph Organization & Flow (handout; Purdue OWL) 32
Rewriting: How to Do Things With Texts (Harris) 21
rheme 17, 18
rhetorical approaches 5–6
rhetorical grammar 1, 16–20, 31, 48, 54, 65–66, 70; instructional sample 105–113, 115–120; sentence-based frameworks 17
Rhetorical Grammar (Kolln) 12, 17
Rhetorical Grammar (Kolln & Gray) 15, 16
rhetorical tradition 5–6; classical rhetoric 5, 7, 90
Rhetorical Traditions and the Teaching of Writing (Knoblauch & Brannon) 6
Rossen-Knill, D. F. 21, 65

Saldaña, J. 44
schema approaches 9–10, 21, 29
Schwegler, R. A. 29
scientific writing 33
Scientific Writing and Communication (Hofmann) 33
Searle, John 21
Sense of Structure, The (Gopen) 68, 70
sensory aspects of writing: sensory approach 81, 92; sensory terms 27, 30, 31; student perspectives on 47, 55, 60
sentence structure 22–23, 52, 57
small text units, student perspectives on 57–60
Sommers, Nancy 29, 58, 70
Speech Acts (Searle) 21
speech and meaning 21
Sperber, D. 21
St. Martin's Handbook, The (Lunsford) 28, 59
Strauss, A. 44
Strunk, W., Jr. 28
student perspectives: audience awareness 55–57; authors'/coding team's methodology 43–49; convergences and divergences 60–61; idea 49–52; organization 52–55; sensory aspects 55; small text units 57–60
student resources 27–35
Style: Lessons in Clarity and Grace (Williams & Bizup) 30–31, 32
Style: Ten Lessons in Clarity and Grace (Williams) 12, 13–14, 15, 16, 22, 23, 25
Swales, J. M. 9, 24, 33
Swan, J. A. 19, 33
systemic functional linguistics (SFL) 14, 16–17, 19, 59, 90–91

theme 2, 15, 17, 18, 45, 46, 49, 51, 56, 67, 69–70, 77, 85, 111
They Say/I Say: The Moves That Matter in Academic Writing (Graff & Birkenstein) 12, 15, 26–27, 28, 58–59, 68
Time's Arrow (Amis) 18
topic 6, 14, 15, 17–18, 22–23, 24, 28, 31, 32, 47, 49–51, 53, 60, 77, 85
transitions 25, 27, 29, 58–59, 71; bridges, logical and verbal 32
Tse, P. 22, 24, 26–27

University of Chicago Writing Program 29
University of Michigan Sweetland Center for Writing 29
University of North Carolina at Chapel Hill 30, 59

Vernacular Eloquence (Elbow) 7, 34, 55
vocabulary 10, 16, 46
voice-based approach 34, 68, 74, 86–87; instructional sample 95–104; *see also* Elbow, Peter

Wardle, E. 11
White, E. B. 28
Williams, J. M. 12–16, 18–19, 22–26, 30–31, 80–82, 86
Wilson, D. 21
writer-based mental process 7
writer-based perspective 4
writer-focused pedagogies 6–7, 60–61
writers: interactions with readers 24; in partnership with readers 4–5
Writer's Reference, A (Hacker & Sommer) 28, 29
Writer's Way, The (Rawlins & Metzger) 22
Writing Center at the University of North Caroline at Chapel Hill, The 30
writing center websites 29–32
Writing Science (Halliday & Martin) 17
Writing With Power (Elbow) 7

Zinsser, W. 28

Taylor & Francis eBooks

www.taylorfrancis.com

A single destination for eBooks from Taylor & Francis with increased functionality and an improved user experience to meet the needs of our customers.

90,000+ eBooks of award-winning academic content in Humanities, Social Science, Science, Technology, Engineering, and Medical written by a global network of editors and authors.

TAYLOR & FRANCIS EBOOKS OFFERS:

- A streamlined experience for our library customers
- A single point of discovery for all of our eBook content
- Improved search and discovery of content at both book and chapter level

REQUEST A FREE TRIAL
support@taylorfrancis.com

For Product Safety Concerns and Information please contact our EU representative GPSR@taylorandfrancis.com
Taylor & Francis Verlag GmbH, Kaufingerstraße 24, 80331 München, Germany